ERIC MASON
NEHEMIAH
FOR YOU

thegoodbook
COMPANY

Nehemiah For You

© Eric Mason, 2022

Published by:
The Good Book Company

thegoodbook.com | thegoodbook.co.uk
thegoodbook.com.au | thegoodbook.co.nz | thegoodbook.co.in

Published in association with the literary agency of Wolgemuth & Associates.

ISBN: 9781784986780

Cover design by Ben Woodcraft | Printed in India

CONTENTS

SERIES PREFACE

Each volume of the *God's Word For You* series takes you to the heart of a book of the Bible, and applies its truths to your heart.

The central aim of each title is to be:

- Bible centered
- Christ glorifying
- Relevantly applied
- Easily readable

You can use *Nehemiah For You:*

To read. You can simply read from cover to cover, as a book that explains and explores the themes, encouragements and challenges of this part of Scripture.

To feed. You can work through this book as part of your own personal regular devotions, or use it alongside a sermon or Bible-study series at your church. Each chapter is divided into two (or occasionally three) shorter sections, with questions for reflection at the end of each.

To lead. You can use this as a resource to help you teach God's word to others, both in small-group and whole-church settings. You'll find tricky verses or concepts explained using ordinary language, and helpful themes and illustrations along with suggested applications.

These books are not commentaries. They assume no understanding of the original Bible languages, nor a high level of biblical knowledge. Verse references are marked in **bold** so that you can refer to them easily. Any words that are used rarely or differently in everyday language outside the church are marked in **gray** when they first appear, and are explained in a glossary toward the back. There, you'll also find details of resources you can use alongside this one, in both personal and church life.

Our prayer is that as you read, you'll be struck not by the contents of this book, but by the book it's helping you open up; and that you'll praise not the author of this book, but the One he is pointing you to.

Carl Laferton, Series Editor

Bible translation used:

ESV: English Standard Version (This is the version being quoted unless otherwise stated.)

NLT: New Living Translation

NIV: New International Version

INTRODUCTION TO NEHEMIAH

Nehemiah is one of those books that can easily end up being hidden from the sight of the believer. It is one of the smaller historical books—like Ezra or Esther—and it tells the story of the rebuilding of the walls of Jerusalem after the people's return from exile. This was a key moment in the history of God's people.

But if we walk away from this book with just a rebuilt wall, we miss many greater things that it's possible to see in the pages of this rich book. It has an obvious relevance to any type of rebuilding we might do for God—from our homes and families to our local churches, communities, cities, and government. It teaches us about **gospel*** mission. We have to be careful not to get locked into the details and fail to see the greater themes of **redemption** and the **providence** of God.

God had a key role for his people, Israel, and that was for them to be **priests** to the nations (Exodus 19:6). That was what Jerusalem was all about: a city on a hill, a light to the world, representing the rule of God. Often, Israel forgot this and fell into selfishness, idolatry, and all-round failure to live up to their **covenant** with God. Sound familiar? We can be this way as well. Nehemiah shows us the work it takes to rebuild representation of the glory of God to the nations.

In Nehemiah we also see that God is ultimately the initiator of his kingdom being built, and we are his divine **stewards** and representatives. When we are in the midst of great need, opposition, rebellion, encumbrances, and sins, God still works through us and motivates us to complete his work.

I can't tell you how many times I've used the book of Nehemiah for leadership development, church-planter training, pastor development, entrepreneurial advice, and personal devotion and encouragement. We can see ourselves and our lives in it. But most of all we can see God's intentions, his glory, and his Son.

---

* Words in **gray** are defined in the Glossary (page 163).

Overview of Nehemiah

The events of Nehemiah took place toward the beginning of what's called the Second Temple Period (around 516 BC – AD 70). God's people had been in captivity, first under the Babylonians and then under the Persians. There were several groups that departed from Persia and returned to Jerusalem to re-establish God's people in their own land. One wave was led by Ezra, another by Zerubbabel, and another by Nehemiah. Ezra was a **scribe**, so he helped with re-educating Israel; Zerubbabel was a priest and re-established the priesthood; and Nehemiah was the governor, who helped with social order. Each had their own place in God's plan.

At the start of the book, Nehemiah finds out about the broken-down condition of Jerusalem and is moved to action. He gains support from the Persian king to get involved in God's plan to re-establish Israel in their own land.

Throughout, we see the enormous courage, zeal, and spiritual resilience of Nehemiah as he seeks to turn this broken city into a light for the nations again. At the center of his activity is the reconstruction and repair of the walls of Jerusalem. The rebuilding of the walls would be a sign that Jerusalem was a city again.

> Nehemiah wanted to turn this broken city into a light for the nations.

But the deepest things that needed to be addressed weren't the structure or aesthetics of the city but the heart of the city. It was the people of God that gave the city its reputation and character. Therefore, Nehemiah began to focus on the social and spiritual character of the people. He dealt with issues of justice, resisted the distractions of enemies, and reinstated the word of God in its place at the center of the life of the city. The focus in chapters 1 to 7 is more on external, physical issues and social renewal. Chapters 8 to 13 focus more on inward, spiritual issues and covenant renewal.

Whether they knew it or not, Nehemiah and the rest were only a few generations from the Savior's coming. Jesus would live, die, and rise again, and would guide the people of God beyond the walls of Jerusalem in mission, to establish his reign over the nations. It's a mission we're still part of today.

1. REBUILT TO BUILD

As we look at the first few verses of Nehemiah, I want to explain how the story connects to the grand theme of what God has been doing, has done, and will do.

Redeemed to Represent

Nehemiah is nestled at the beginning of what's called the Second Temple Period, when the **temple** was being rebuilt in Jerusalem and the people of God were returning from exile.

Long before that, God had chosen the Israelites to be his own people, to show off who he was to the world. Deuteronomy 7:6-7 explains this:

> "The LORD your God has chosen you to be a people for his trea-
> sured possession, out of all the peoples who are on the face of
> the earth. It was not because you were more in number than
> any other people that the LORD set his love on you and chose
> you, for you were the fewest of all people."

God likes to choose people that have nothing—that are unimpressive. They are "the fewest of all peoples." Paul says a similar thing about the Christian church in 1 Corinthians 1:26: "Not many of you were wise according to worldly standards, not many were powerful, not many were of noble birth." God hasn't chosen just the cool people. Some of us are geeks. Some of us are awkward. Some of us are weird. All of us are sinful. But God is going to use these weaknesses, because people know we're like that, and so, as God transforms us and makes us look more like himself, people will realize that there's something about us that is beyond us.

All Christians are God's people now, but initially God chose the people of Israel to display who he was to the other nations (Isaiah 49:8-9; 60:1-3). And this was to happen in a particular place: the **promised land**, and specifically in the city of Jerusalem. Deuteronomy 12:5 says, "You shall seek the place that the Lord your God will choose out of all your tribes to put his name and make his habitation there." Jerusalem was the place where God's presence dwelt. It was the center of the whole nation, the center of their worship, the center of their representation of him. This was why being sent away into exile, away from Jerusalem, was such a terrible thing.

Exile was initiated because of the people's disobedience. God had given his people this mission, and they had failed him by becoming idolaters. (Idolatry is worshiping anyone or anything instead of God.) Whenever anything gets in the place where God should be in the life of his people, he first calls them to repentance. He did that in this case through his prophets—Isaiah and others. But if they don't repent, he pulls out a cosmic belt. God disciplines his children because he loves them. The Babylonians, under the rule of Nebuchadnezzar, besieged Jerusalem during the reign of Jehoiachin—around 597 BC. They took the people of **Judah** into captivity. Later, the Persians came in and took over; they took Babylon itself into captivity, together with all the nations that the Babylonians had taken into captivity.

For the Israelites, exile did not just involve the pain of moving and being uncertain about the future; there was also the pain of being taken away from the place where God was and where they were supposed to be representing him.

Even in the midst of this discipline, however, God's people were still to represent his name. He told them through the prophet Jeremiah, "Seek the welfare of the city where I have sent you into exile, and pray to the LORD on its behalf, for in its welfare you will find your welfare" (Jeremiah 29:7). That's one thing that's beautiful about the God of heaven: whenever he gets after someone, he gets after them with purpose.

He tells us this in the New Testament as well. Ephesians 2:8 says, "By **grace** you have been saved through faith." Then verse 10 goes on, "We are his workmanship, created in Christ Jesus for good works, which God prepared beforehand, that we should walk in them."

In other words, God's people are redeemed to represent. "Redeemed" means "bought back." He saves us, and then he **anoints** us to represent him. That's a broad Bible principle; the mission of God through his people is rooted in our identity in him. We are redeemed to represent. God's people of all times have always been called to represent his reign on earth.

Back to Jerusalem

Through the prophet Jeremiah, God had told his people, "I know the plans I have for you … plans for welfare and not for evil, to give you a future and a hope" (Jeremiah 29:11). Even in the middle of the discipline he was giving them, he offered them comfort and purpose.

God intervened so that the king of Persia (Cyrus the Great and then his successors) allowed the people to go back to Jerusalem and rebuild the temple and the city. There were three waves of return to Jerusalem—led by Zerubbabel, Ezra, and then Nehemiah. The books of Ezra and Nehemiah describe these returns, but they are not attempting to provide a complete detailed history of this 100-year-plus time span. Instead they focus on only a few highly significant years (see Gregory Goswell, "Ezra-Nehemiah," in *The Baker Illustrated Bible Background Commentary*, ed. J. Scott Duvall and J. Daniel Hays, p 371). That's why there are chronological gaps between Ezra 6 and 7, between Ezra 10 and Nehemiah 1, and between Nehemiah 13:3 and 13:4.

The word Nehemiah means "**Yahweh** comforts." Isn't that beautiful? Isn't that something? Who else gives you a whipping, and then comforts you? Through Nehemiah, through Ezra, and through the prophets God sent at this time—Malachi, Haggai, Zephaniah and Zechariah—God was encouraging his people and giving them hope. He was saying, *It's all right now. It hurt, didn't it? But I just did it* *because I love you.* That's the way God is; he comforts his people after he disciplines them. This is important because when the people of Judah get back to Jerusalem and see the state of the city, they are going to need comfort.

Among those who have already returned to Jerusalem is Hanani, the brother of Nehemiah. He and all of the returned exiles are feeling broken about the circumstances and condition of the city to which God has sent them. Hanani goes back to Susa, which was the capital of Persia, and he comes to see Nehemiah (Nehemiah **1:2***).

Nehemiah asks him questions about the Jews who are in Jerusalem, and about the state of the city itself. This is Hanani's response: "The remnant there in the province who had survived the exile is in great trouble and shame. The wall of Jerusalem is broken down, and its gates are destroyed by fire."

There is only a remnant of the people still left in the city. That means a small group of people that God has drafted to continue to represent him.

But this remnant is "in great trouble and shame" (**v 3**), and the wall of Jerusalem has been broken down. The city walls had been destroyed by Nebuchadnezzar, and despite some attempts to rebuild them, they remained in ruins for almost a century and a half. Such a lamentable situation obviously made Jerusalem vulnerable to numerous enemies. Yet because of a mixture of apathy and fear, the Jews had failed to rectify this glaring deficiency. Archaeologist Kathleen Kenyon notes:

"The effect on Jerusalem was much more disastrous and far-reaching than merely to render the city defenseless ... The whole system of terraces down the (eastern) slope, dependent on retaining walls buttressed in turn by the fill of the next lower terrace, was ultimately dependent on the town wall at the base, forming the lowest and most substantial of the retaining walls." (*Digging up Jerusalem*, p 170)

---

* All Nehemiah verse references being looked at in each chapter part are in **bold**.

In other words, the whole integrity of the city was threatened by the broken-down state of the walls. It's no surprise that the people felt wrecked and without help.

My older sister was right outside the Pentagon on 9/11 when the plane crashed into it. She told me about the look on people's faces walking around that day. It was as if you could see the rubble and the dust in their eyes. There was desperation and there was broken-ness because of what they had seen. It wasn't just the US defense headquarters that had been broken down. People's own defenses had been, too. That's the same kind of brokenness that Nehemiah saw on his brother's face.

But this remnant of God's people in Jerusalem was not only dis-traught because of the physical destruction. As we know, Jerusalem was always about something bigger than just being a beautiful city or a well-defended one. It was the dwelling place of God. The reason why there was such pain among those who had returned from exile was that the representation of God by his people had waned.

The book of Nehemiah is the story of how it was built back up again.

The City in the City

This all applies to us as followers of Jesus Christ because we are God's people now—the ones who represent him to the world. In fact, Jesus compares us to a city in Matthew 5:14.

"You are the light of the world. A city set on a hill cannot be hidden."

A city isn't merely the geography; a city is a people. We are a city set on a hill, like Jerusalem. That's why Revelation 21:2-3 talks about a new Jerusalem. "I saw the holy city, new Jerusalem, coming down out of heaven from God, prepared as a bride adorned for her husband. And I heard a loud voice from the throne saying, 'Behold, the dwell-ing place of God is with man. He will dwell with him, and they will be his people, and God himself will be with them as their God." This is what we as the church are going to be like one day: a new city, a new Jerusalem, where God dwells.

> We're like movie trailers for that city— the place every community is supposed to look like.

This eternal Jerusalem is going to have no mourning, no crying, no dying, and no pain (v 4). No deprivation or injustice or crime. It is going to be the cleanest city ever! That is what cities look like when God runs them. The new Jerusalem is the archetypal city: the community that every community is ultimately supposed to look like. And God wants us to be like movie trailers for that city. God has redeemed us, and that means that he wants us to be his representatives in the places that he has sent us into.

Missiologist Lois Barrett helpfully explains what that means:

"Key images of God's alternative community, the missional church, are found in the Gospels' descriptions of the people of God as 'the salt of the earth,' a 'light of the world,' and a 'city set on a hill.' These images suggest that mission is not just what the church does; it is what the church is. Saltiness is not an action; it is the very character of salt. Similarly, light or a city on a hill need not do anything in order to be seen. So too it is with God's 'people sent.' The visible, taste-able nature of their community is their missional purpose: by encountering that 'holy nation,' others 'may see your good works and give glory to your Father in heaven' (Matthew 5:16)."

(in Darrell L. Guder, *Missional Church*, p 128)

What God is helping us to think through in Nehemiah is this: what does it look like to see the power of the gospel transform and rebuild us into a reflection of the eternal Jerusalem? And how is that going to change the world? God calls us to proclaim his gospel in the world so that people's lives can be changed holistically. We want to see a reflection of the beauty of the new Jerusalem. We long to see no more mourning or crying or pain in the lives of the people we live among. We're trying to see comprehensive gospel change. That is what Nehemiah is about.

On Mission

It is time to rebuild. It is time to join God on mission—to join what he has been doing since the **fall**. The world is in trouble, and he has sent us in as his special ops team. We need all hands on deck because this is a war. In Jesus' name, it is time to get out there. That's what it means to be on mission.

Too many Christians are just consumers. We say, "I need a word about this... I need God to help me with that... I need..." No! God wants us to do something for his glory in our neighborhoods. We've got to roll up our sleeves. No more consumerism.

Of course, you and I do need things. We need the word of God. We need to worship together. We need good **theology**. But when Acts 2:42 says, "They devoted themselves to the **apostles**' teaching," it means not just hearing it but executing it. If church becomes about what we can get, we're doing it wrong. We have been redeemed in order to represent God together to the people around us.

Here's how Nehemiah responds to his brother's news. "I sat down and wept and mourned for days, and I continued **fasting** and praying before the God of heaven" (Nehemiah **1:4**).

A verse like that prompts us to ask questions of ourselves. Have I wept? Have I mourned for the state of God's people? Have I mourned for the state of the world? Have I felt the brokenness Nehemiah felt? Remember, the people in Jerusalem in Nehemiah's time were "in great trouble and shame." That word "trouble" means "brokenness"—being smashed, being injured, being absolutely shattered by circumstances.

That is what God has called us into. He has not called us into a pretty ministry. He wants us to care so much about his kingdom that we are broken when we don't see his rule represented as it should be.

He wants us to get on our faces and cry out to him. We should be expectant, believing in Jesus' name that God is going to work in our communities. But he is not going to do it apart from us, the people he has redeemed to represent him.

Questions for reflection

1. How do you respond to the idea that we are redeemed to represent God in the world?

2. What brokenness do you see in the church and in the world around you? What could you do to represent God in those situations?

3. Where have you seen consumerist attitudes in church? How can you guard against this kind of attitude?

PART TWO

At the start of chapter 2, Nehemiah will take action and go before the king. But first, he prays.

The period of time when he was praying was four months—from the Hebrew month of Chislev (**1:1**), which is our November and December, to the month of Nisan (2:1), which is in March and April. For those four months Nehemiah prayed and fasted. Fasting in this situation is an expression of sorrow over the failings of God's people and their resulting distress (see also Ezra 10:6; Nehemiah 9:1). It is also a movement in the direction of the needed change, since it means walking in faith. Before Nehemiah did anything else, he said, *I'm going to seek God about this.* He was crying out to God and expecting him to work.

Prayer is not about us dictating our own will to God. People can't twist God's arm. Prayer is a way of aligning ourselves with his will. It is submission to the **sovereignty** of God. We are asking God to release from heaven onto the earth what he has already decided to do. That does not mean it's pointless to pray: God uses prayer. He wants us to relate to him and ask him for things. Prayer is the interpersonal, in-depth interaction between God and his covenant people. It is a way of enjoying him and of seeing him active on our planet.

There have been many times in my life when I wish I had shut my mouth to people and opened my mouth to God. Prayer would have changed the situation, and it would have changed my disposition! That's what we see in Nehemiah 1: encountering God in prayer is vital if you want to see rebuilding in your life and in the world around you.

But it is important to note that the encounter with God that Nehemiah seeks is not for his own sake alone. He wants to see a unified community encountering God together. His encounter with God is for others.

Recognizing Who God Is

Usually when I'm going through something difficult, when I come to prayer, I say things like "God, I'm sick of..." or "God, I'm tired of..." Or I just say, "Help!" But look at how Nehemiah starts his prayer in Nehemiah **1:5**: "O LORD God of heaven." What a beautiful statement to make! The first part of Nehemiah's prayer is a recognition of who God is. He is focusing on the transcendence of God—the fact that he is far above and beyond all things. Nehemiah is reminding himself that God is sovereign over all creation; his rule is comprehensive. God is the boss! And this isn't merely about how high God is in his nature but also about the place he is in. God is in the heavenly realm. In saying this, Nehemiah is clear that the natural problems that confront him are rooted in spiritual issues. This is a supernatural statement.

Nehemiah is putting his mind beyond his circumstance. In prayer we must do that. If we focus our minds on our own brokenness, we'll stay in it. But if we zoom in on the God of heaven, we'll get beyond it. "Seek the things that are above, where Christ is," Paul tells us in Colossians 3:1. Wherever you are, whatever your circumstances, you'd better look at God, who is over it all.

Nehemiah knows that he is under an earthly king. He has an earthly boss. He is going to go and see him at the start of the next chapter. But first he wants to talk to the one who runs everything. He is trying to get his heart postured heavenward because he knows that that brings earthly transformation. Likewise, if anything in our own lives is going to be changed, and if anything in our communities is going to be changed, all of the people of God should be pointed heavenward. We have to point to the one who is above all things—the God of heaven. He alone has the ability to control, and not to be controlled, by any circumstance.

Nehemiah goes on: "the great and awesome God" (Nehemiah **1:5**). This is called a *hendiadys*: two words put next to one another to express a single idea more forcefully. God is both "great" and "awesome." The combination gives potency to Nehemiah's meaning, showing just how high he believes God is.

The word "great" here is not a throwaway word, like saying, "Great job, buddy." It means "important." It means a high status. It can also mean "strange" in the sense of causing astonishment (see Exodus 3:3): God supersedes what is normal and natural. He is uniquely great beyond everything. Nehemiah is talking to the miraculous God.

Meanwhile, the word "awesome" is the Hebrew word *yaray*, which means "to fear." This word points to the idea of standing in awe of the reality of God: taking God seriously and fearing his power and might.

Put the two together and we see that Nehemiah is talking about standing in awe of the reality of the one who supersedes the natural. That is who Nehemiah is praying to: the all-powerful, **transcendent** God.

> God supersedes what is normal and natural. He is beyond everything.

But not only is God transcendent; he is also immanent. That means he breaks into circumstances. The old preachers would say that he sits high, but he looks low. He is the God "who keeps covenant and steadfast love." The word translated "steadfast love" is *hesed*. Nehemiah is talking about God's graciousness, his goodness, his loyal love, and his faithfulness. *Hesed* is an almost untranslatable word—it means all those things at once! Here, the most important aspect of it is God's loyalty to his people. God is more loyal than a mother. He has chosen his people, and he sticks by them. They seem to be the most trifling people on the planet, but God is loyal to them.

Nehemiah is setting his prayer up. He is naming the **attributes** of God that he is going to need. He starts by saying, *God, you know you. You know you are powerful and loyal.* Then he will ask God to act based on those characteristics.

God likes it when we pray like that. He likes it when we put faith in who he is in order to show off what he does. That's the way he works.

Confessing Sin

Besides acknowledging who God is, we also have to acknowledge who we are. That is why Nehemiah goes on in his prayer to confess the people's sin (Nehemiah **1:6-7**).

The church needs to hear about sin. We cannot just talk about purpose—getting out and getting up and going into a new season. We are not going to be rebuilt to go anywhere until God deals with our mess. And it is some mess! But, as Christians, we get to deal with our mess with hope. "If we confess our sins, he is faithful and just to forgive us our sins and to cleanse us from all unrighteousness" (1 John 1:9).

Nehemiah is praying on behalf of his whole nation and asking for forgiveness for generations of sin (Nehemiah **1:6**). He was not even alive when this sin began. But he is confessing it as a participant in it, because he has benefited from and possibly walked in the sins of his forefathers. He is not blaming anybody else. He goes ahead and confesses all of that sin himself.

This is even plainer in the last two phrases of **verse 6**. He is confessing the sins "which we have sinned against you." He goes from "we"—a plural pronoun that includes himself but also others—to pronouns that indicate individual, personal responsibility: "Even I and my father's house have sinned."

This has an obvious application in the US for our current culture of racial unrest. We must understand the impact of multigenerational sin and the systemic nature of its impact. With any multigenerational sin, there can be a legacy that reaches and affects future generations. From sexual sin to family idolatry, we must be willing to own our connection to any sin that is overtly or covertly present in our generation, and the ways we may have benefited from its consequences.

What is this multigenerational sin in Nehemiah's case? In **verse 7** he says that he and his people have acted not just corruptly but "very corruptly"—and this against God himself. They "have not kept the commandments, the statutes, and the rules that you commanded your servant Moses."

When God rescued his people out of Egypt, he promised to be their God, and they promised to be his people. They promised to keep the law that he had given them for their good (Exodus 24:3). But they have not kept that law. Nehemiah acknowledges that they have been comprehensively unfaithful.

The Hebrew word for "confess" in Nehemiah **1:6** means to throw or cast something down. This is not gently laying your sin at God's feet. It means throwing down your sin before God like a volleyball: spiking it before the King with all your strength. If we want God to use us, that's how we need to confess. We must not just say, "Well, all I did was..." or "It wasn't entirely my fault" or "If they hadn't done that, I wouldn't have..." or "I'm not directly doing anything wrong." That is not repentance. That means we are still trying to conceal our wrongdoing. Instead we should say, "This is my sin." In other words, tell God everything. Ask him to expose all the sin in you. Why? Because it is by tearing yourself down that you will let God rebuild you.

Praying God's Word

Nehemiah has acknowledged God's attributes and the people's sin, and next he acknowledges the truth of God's word. In fact, Nehemiah has already been praying God's word back to him, when he confessed that the people had not kept God's laws (**v 7**). Now he says, "Remember the word that you commanded your servant Moses" (**v 8**).

The best thing we can do when we pray is to pray God's word back to him—asking him to act on what he has promised to do in his word. Nehemiah is saying, *I'm just telling you what you said, God!*

God said to Moses, "If you are unfaithful, I will scatter you among the peoples" (**v 8**). This is not an exact quotation but a paraphrase of something God has said numerous times—for example, in Deuteronomy 4:25-27. That is exactly the situation Nehemiah is in right now; God has taken his people out of their land and scattered them. So Nehemiah is living in the truth of God's word by default!

But scattering is not the only thing that God promised to Moses. He went on, "But if you return to me and keep my commandments and do them..." In other words, God had commanded them to go back to Jerusalem and, as God's people, to represent him again. This was God's promise: "Though your outcasts are in the uttermost parts of heaven, from there I will gather them and bring them to the place that I have chosen, to make my name dwell there" (Nehemiah **1:9**; see Deuteronomy 30:1-4; 12:5). If the people repented of their sin and turned back to God, then God would bring them back to Jerusalem and give them his presence again. In returning to Jerusalem, Ezra, Nehemiah, and Zerubbabel were acting on that promise. They were being faithful to the word of God.

God would make his name dwell with them—that is, the name Yahweh. For us, God has taken the name Yahweh and inserted it into the name of Jesus (or, in Hebrew, Yashua):

"God has highly exalted him and bestowed on him the name that is above every name, so that at the name of Jesus every knee should bow, in heaven and on earth and under the earth, and every tongue confess that Jesus Christ is Lord, to the glory of God the Father." (Philippians 2:9-11)

"Lord" here is the Greek word "kyrios," which is a translation of the name "Yahweh." So Jesus fulfills what it means for God to dwell among his people. He literally came to dwell among us (John 1:14). And he dwells with us still: if you are a believer, you have Christ in you. He "dwell[s] in your hearts through faith" (Ephesians 3:17). By his Spirit, he lives in and among us—within the body of believers. We have unending, uninterrupted fellowship with the living God.

God no longer disciplines us by shipping us out of our land. Now the discipline of the Lord is done by the Holy Spirit in our hearts. He may make you very uncomfortable simply by showing you your own sin. But this is a sign that he is moving in your heart to turn you back to Jesus.

Nehemiah goes on reminding God of his word—next recounting what he has already done for his people. He is referring to the **exodus** when he says, "They are your servants and your people, whom you have redeemed by your great power and by your strong hand" (Nehemiah **1:10**).

In Hebrew thought, your "hands" include your forearms. So it is interesting that Nehemiah says that God has delivered his people by his "strong hand"—because in Isaiah 53:1-3, the "arm of the Lord" is a prophecy of Jesus. This is a reminder that ultimately Jesus brings deliverance. Nobody else. God is not working through anybody but Jesus.

Asking in Faith

Only at this point does Nehemiah make his request to the Lord. "O Lord, let your ear be attentive to the prayer of your servant, and to the prayer of your servants who delight to fear your name" (Nehemiah **1:11**). Then he specifically asks God to give him success in what he is about to do: to "grant him mercy in the sight of this man."

Artaxerxes, the king of Persia, was seen by his people as a god. When Nehemiah goes before him in the next chapter, he will say, "Let the king live forever!" (2:3). He has to go in like that. But in private prayer beforehand he calls the king "this man." The phrase "this man" is pejorative and disrespectful. That's the force of the language. After all, Artaxerxes is just a man, and Nehemiah is before God. No matter what this man is doing in Nehemiah's life, Nehemiah recognizes that "The king's heart is a stream of water in the hand of the LORD; he turns it wherever he will" (Proverbs 21:1).

You and I should recognize the same thing. No matter where we are in life, no human is sovereign over it. No human has power like God's.

Remember, circumstances are what they are: circumstantial. They are temporary. But the King of kings is transcendent, yet immanent—over our circumstances and, at the same time, in our circumstances. There is nothing that God does not see. Because we are in Christ, he is in us.

The chapter finishes with Nehemiah saying, "Now I was cupbearer to the king" (Nehemiah **1:11**). In other words, Nehemiah is going to leverage his position for God's exaltation. Nehemiah is about to go and ask the king to help his people, and he is going by faith. He started this prayer mourning. But now something is different about him. He is ready to go before the king.

Questions for reflection

1. What strikes you the most about Nehemiah's prayer? Is there anything you'd like to change about your own prayers?

2. How often do you confess your sin to God? Why is this such a good and vital thing to do?

3. How can knowing the Bible help us to pray?

2. NEHEMIAH MAKES PLANS

Whether you're studying or in business, whether you're an hourly worker or salaried or unemployed, whether you live in the city center or on a remote farm—in other words, no matter where you find yourself—you are on a journey with God through Jesus Christ. In light of that, each of us has to recognize that God has put us where we are right now for a particular purpose. That changes the way we view ourselves being there. We can like being there or we can dislike being there, but we can't forget that God has put us there. Wherever we're going and wherever we are, God has placed us there for him.

Nehemiah is the cupbearer to the king (1:11). That is where God has put him. In chapter 2, he leverages that position for God's purposes.

Divine Courage

The chapter begins, "In the month of Nisan, in the twentieth year of King Artaxerxes, when wine was before him..." (**2:1**).

We seem to be in the Persian version of Mardi Gras. The Persian kings were famous for their drinking parties (see Esther 1:3-8), which were an ancient custom in the Near East. This is a festive time. There is drinking and dancing and feasting. People are enjoying themselves. And Nehemiah, a Jew, is the cupbearer to the king. He is basically the king's personal bartender. So he's standing there in the middle of the party, pouring drinks for Artaxerxes.

Nehemiah is free to enjoy the king's court, but he sees his place there as being about something bigger than enjoyment. He is at the right hand of Artaxerxes. He sees himself as a missional figure, placed in a particular role at a particular time for a particular purpose: for the glory of God.

In fact, he is not enjoying himself at all. And not just because he's at work! At this point Nehemiah has been praying for four months. He's been fasting. He has been coming before God with a broken heart. Now, finally, we see him beginning to leverage his position.

Until this point, Nehemiah says, "I had not been sad in [the king's] presence" (Nehemiah **2:1**). That shows us something. In Nehemiah's day, you didn't come before the king sad. You'd run the risk of getting your head chopped off! Persian works of art, such as the great treasury reliefs from Persepolis, indicate that those who came into the king's presence did so with great deference, placing the right hand with palm facing the mouth so as not to defile the king with one's breath (see John H. Walton, *Zondervan Illustrated Bible Backgrounds Commentary: Old Testament,* volume 3, p 424). Coming before the king was a serious business.

But now Nehemiah was in the king's presence, and he was visibly sad—so much so that the king asked why (**v 2**).

What was going through Artaxerxes' mind? The fact that the king was able to distinguish between physical illness and mental concern ("Why is your face so sad, seeing you are not sick?") is an indication that Artaxerxes had a close relationship with his cupbearer and knew him well. But was he just concerned for his servant? Perhaps he was wary: a cupbearer's worried demeanor might make him fear an assassination attempt. Or maybe he was angry: why should his cupbearer spoil the party? Literally, Artaxerxes' question is "Why is your face so bad?" The word translated "sad" has a great variety of meanings but is always associated with something unpleasant, bad, or wicked.

Nehemiah gives us a clue as to Artaxerxes' attitude toward him when he tells us, "I was very much afraid." He knew that something terrible might happen, and he was shaken.

Yet Nehemiah was choosing to risk his life because of his passion for God's kingdom. He wanted to leverage this opportunity that he had before the king.

A Wise Interaction

Nehemiah used his words wisely. He started with respect: "Let the king live forever!" (**v 3**). Then he said, "Why should not my face be sad, when the city, the place of my fathers' graves, lies in ruins, and its gates have been destroyed by fire?"

He said, "the place of my fathers' graves" instead of "Jerusalem" because he wanted Artaxerxes to connect emotionally. Back then, family legacy was very important. Artaxerxes wouldn't understand that Jerusalem was God's city, but he could imagine that you would want your ancestral city, where your family had lived for generations, to look nice. In other words, Nehemiah was contextualizing the information for Artaxerxes, in order to persuade him to help. This is a lesson in how to wisely engage with unbelievers. We find common ground.

One of my "sons in the ministry," who pastors a church that we planted in Camden, NJ, used breeding dogs as a means to develop common ground with people in his community. He wrote:

"Our common interest in dog breeding has provided a starting point of discussion with people who would not ordinarily want to associate with a church pastoral team. One such person was a young man named Kevin. Kevin, as we came to find out, had been a major drug dealer in the city, but he had recently begun breeding bullies. We quickly formed a bond with him through our dogs. Slowly, we were able to discuss spiritual matters and convinced him to come to church. He came to meet Jesus two years later, and I am proud to say that he has turned his life around. His story has become a powerful witness to the gospel and its transformative truth."

(Doug Logan, *On the Block*, p 171-172)

Colossians 4:5-6 exhorts us to "walk in wisdom toward outsiders … Let your speech always be gracious, seasoned with salt." It isn't necessary for Christians to do big dramatic things to reach the lost. Don't go on a self-righteous rant. Speak wisely to others and try to understand their context. Do an ordinary job that will give you common ground with unbelievers. Share the good news as God opens up doors to do so rather than shouting people down with the gospel. After all, the Holy Spirit doesn't have a bazooka to blow everyone up.

In Luke 16:8, Jesus says something about this: "The sons of this world are more shrewd in dealing with their own generation than the sons of light." He has been talking about an unjust manager who fiddled everybody's bills for them so that, when he was eventually fired, they would let him live with them. Jesus says that this man was shrewd. He didn't operate rightly, but he was shrewd. He used his resources for the best possible outcome for himself. Jesus goes on to say that he wants us to be shrewd, too: to utilize even unrighteous (or worldly, NLT) wealth for kingdom good. The people of God are supposed to leverage all our resources as wisely as we can—not for this life, like the dishonest manager, but for eternity.

That is what Nehemiah does. He is shrewd in the way he deals with Artaxerxes, for the honor of God and the glory of God. He wants to utilize this opportunity in a beautiful way. He gives his answer very carefully and gently. The result is that the king is ready to listen. "What are you requesting?" he says (Nehemiah **2:4**).

Prayer and Planning

Before Nehemiah replies, he again prays "to the God of heaven" (**v 4**). He is in this situation with Artaxerxes, but he recognizes that there is a king better than Artaxerxes. So he goes into what some people call "staccato prayer"—just a quick, silent prayer while he's standing there. He doesn't start crying out, "O God!" in front of Artaxerxes. But he does go into prayer, asking for God's help with what he is about to say.

Finally, he continues—after all, kings are not patient people. Nehemiah is submissive in the way he addresses Artaxerxes: "If it pleases the king, and if your servant has found favor in your sight..." He's pouring it on thick! Then he makes his request. He asks to be sent to Judah (**v 5**).

But that's not all he says. In the following verses we see that Nehemiah has already made meticulous plans. He knows exactly what he needs from the king.

Artaxerxes asks how long Nehemiah would be gone (**v 6**). Nehemiah is ready with an answer. The journey from Susa, which was the capital of Persia, down to Jerusalem was one of 900 miles. What with all the baggage that they needed to carry, and the animals to transport it, it would have taken four months to get there and four months to get back. Nehemiah had to give the king the time it was going to take for him to go there, get the work started and finished, and return. So he probably gave a time period of well over a year.

The king is going to lose his cupbearer for more than a year. But he agrees. Think about that! Nobody gets a year off, just like that. This has to be God at work.

Next Nehemiah gets bold. He is courageous because he knows he is working on God's behalf. So he now asks the king for protection: "Let letters be given me to the governors of the province Beyond the River, that they may let me pass through" (**v 7**).

The idea of the letters was that Nehemiah would show them to those whose territory he was entering so that they wouldn't attack him or his people. He had to make sure he had the king's letters with him to show he was on official business. In other words, Nehemiah was prepared for all hell to break loose. He realized that there was going to be opposition, and he wanted to be ready for it.

Christians throughout the ages have encountered opposition. *The Passion of St Perpetua and St Felicity*, written in the 3rd century, tells how Perpetua, a Christian from North Africa, and her slave Felicity, along with other African believers, were imprisoned and, after their baptism, condemned to execution in the arena at Carthage. They were willing to stand for Jesus and the gospel even to the point of death. Stories like this remind us that the people of God should expect opposition when representing the reign of God. Nehemiah will get his safe passage into the land, as we will see. However, once he gets there, he will need spiritual fortitude to be fruitful and faithful amid fanatical opponents of God's work.

As we seek to build God's kingdom, we too will come up against hostility and difficulty. We need to recognize it and prepare for it. That's why Peter said, "Do not be surprised at the fiery **trial** when it comes upon you" (1 Peter 4:12). That's why Paul and Barnabas said, "Through many tribulations we must enter the kingdom of God" (Acts 14:22). The people of God have to recognize that opposition is going to happen. People hated Jesus; they will hate us too.

Jesus told us to count the cost of discipleship in advance. "Which of you, desiring to build a tower, does not first sit down and count the cost, whether he has enough to complete it?" (Luke 14:28). It is the same with the Christian life. If we follow Jesus, there is going to be loss. We need to be ready for that, just as Nehemiah was.

Nehemiah is not finished with his requests to Artaxerxes. He also says he wants "a letter to Asaph, the keeper of the king's forest, that he may give me timber" (Nehemiah **2:8**). The king has a forest. He has acres and acres and acres of land. And Nehemiah wants to use that wood—so that he can do the work not out of Judah's budget but out of the king's own budget. Nehemiah wasn't using this timber to line his own pocket. He was going to use it for the building of the walls and whatever else was needed. Yes, he was also going to build himself a house (**v 8**)—but he told Artaxerxes that. There was no double dealing here.

Can you imagine saying this kind of thing to your boss? "Number one, I want a year off. Number two, I need a reference letter because I'm going to be taking another job while I'm away. And number three, I'd like you to finance the whole project." It's crazy talk.

But it is also a lesson to us. We have to courageously use whatever role we have been given to build God's kingdom. For example, there's an assistant district attorney in our church who is leveraging her role in the city to help the church bridge the gap between the police and black communities for long-term peace and understanding. Then there are the home-schooling moms in our church who, in the midst of the COVID-19 pandemic, helped other parents who had never home-schooled before to make sense of how to help their children get through the year—again, building friendships and bridges for the sake of the gospel.

Be courageous in reaching out! All people can say is no. But don't just walk in there with no prayer and no plan. Nehemiah prayed and planned for four months before he said anything to the king.

The king grants Nehemiah what he asks. But here's a final thing to note. Nehemiah doesn't say that he got what he wanted because he was gifted or because he was persuasive or because he had planned meticulously or even because he had been diligent in prayer. He tells us, "The good hand of my God was upon me" (**v 8**). God sometimes seems like he's in the background in the book of Nehemiah—he does not speak—but he is deeply active. After all, he is the executive producer of everything that happens on earth, seen and unseen. God is actively involved. Nehemiah knows this.

> The surest way to experience God's helping hands is to seek his heart first.

The surest way to experience God's helping hands is to seek his heart first. We have to be in his presence. We have to be spending time with him. We have to be hearing hard sayings from him. We have to repent of sin. Nehemiah did all that in chapter 1, and now God has put his hand on him. God is using Nehemiah for his glory as Nehemiah seeks to leverage his life for God.

Questions for reflection

1. Think about a person or group you are trying to reach with the gospel. What could you do to build common ground with them?

2. How might Nehemiah's shrewdness translate to your situation?

3. How could you encourage those around you to be courageous in prayer and in working for God's kingdom?

PART TWO

When you have a dream or a vision to do something, you develop plans, goals, and objectives to help you to reach that particular dream. But as you begin to get into the grime and the grit of the process, although the vision may not change, the specific way you plan to get there does change. You become more aware of the situation you are in, and that awareness impacts how you plan. It is good to have a sense of calling, but it is no good to be unrealistic about what it is going to look like to walk into that calling.

Nehemiah has made careful plans already, but as he heads to Jerusalem, we see how his awareness of the situation changes, and what impact that has on what he does.

Ready for Obstacles

"The province Beyond the River" (**v 9**) was the whole geographical area between the River Euphrates and the Mediterranean Sea, roughly equivalent to modern Syria, Jordan, Palestine, and Israel, as well as parts of Iraq. So, Nehemiah has arrived. He is almost ready to begin the process of rebuilding the wall of Jerusalem. But God gives him the grace to know that there is going to be opposition all the way through the process.

Nehemiah has already prepared for opposition by asking the king for letters, but now he knows who the hostility is actually going to come from: Sanballat the Horonite and Tobiah the Ammonite. When these men heard of what Nehemiah was doing, "it displeased them greatly" (**v 10**).

Nehemiah had an army with him besides these letters from the king (**v 9**). So the majority of the people he met must have given him their full support. It is not surprising, then, that Sanballat was frustrated. He was the governor over the region. He must have felt that Nehemiah was infringing upon his authority. Tobiah the Ammonite also seems to have been a leader of the people, but he was on a lower rung than Sanballat. He had been appointed by the king as a servant in this province. So far these two have ignored the state of the city of Jerusalem. But now that Nehemiah had come in to do some work, they woke up. Look at what they were really angry about: "It displeased them greatly that someone had come to seek the welfare of the people of Israel" (**v 10**). This word "welfare" simply means the betterment of someone (see Jeremiah 29:3-7)—just putting people in basic better conditions. Sanballat and Tobiah didn't like the fact that Nehemiah actually wanted to look out for people.

When someone is concerned about what God is concerned about, it's going to ruffle things up. We have to be aware of that reality before we start.

Tweaking Plans

Nehemiah arrives in Jerusalem and rests for three days (Nehemiah **2:11**). Then he acts; he gets up in the night along with a few others, ready to survey the city (**v 12**). But he says, "I told no one what my God had put into my heart to do for Jerusalem." He is showing discretion. He knows when and who to tell what and why—protecting himself from any possible blunders and their consequences.

It's interesting to note Nehemiah's confidence about his vision for rebuilding Jerusalem. He calls it "what God had put into my heart to do." He sees his mission as a God-inspired work. Vision and calling should never be disconnected from the heart and mind of God. Prophetic vision (Proverbs 29:18) means a revelation based on what God has already said—not a revelation based on a personal dream. This is why Paul tells us to test and weigh prophecies (1 Corinthians 14:29; 1 Thessalonians 5:19-22). If we believe we have a calling from God, we should test it in light of what God has already said in the Bible—like Nehemiah's plans, which were based on prayer and on what he had read in God's word. He even quoted God's word back to him (Nehemiah 1:8-9)! So he has utter confidence in this vision. He knows it is God working through him.

At the same time, he does not want to over-promise and under-deliver. If he carries out his plans without testing them in real life, he may turn out to be deluding himself. Nehemiah has heard about the walls and prayed about the condition of the people, but he hasn't yet seen it all for himself. So he stays quiet about his vision for now until he can make himself aware of the precise situation in Jerusalem.

When we were planting the church in Philadelphia where I am the pastor, our plans ended up looking totally different than what we had expected. We had a vision which we believe came from God; our plan to execute this vision was to rent a place—maybe to meet in a school. But God gave us our own building. We never planned to buy—nobody had any money! But God had different plans. He expanded our plans, because he wanted to do what he wanted to do through us more than we wanted to be used by him to do it. After all, he was the initiator of it.

That's why it is important not to confuse vision with plans. God may give you a vision for something in particular, and you will begin executing that vision. In serving a broken community, there will be a lot of practical ways in which you will want to help. One could be economic development. We began to work with people on education in order to move them to economic development, but we soon realized that they had some very practical things missing. We found that people didn't have social security cards or ID. Without these, we couldn't help them legitimately move forward. So we changed our plans and worked on that first. Getting closer to the place where you want to apply your vision gives you awareness—which may make you realize that you need to tweak the plan in order to bring the vision to fruition.

When God doesn't do things your way, you may think that it's the vision God has an issue with. Sometimes it is, and we should weigh up whether it really is in line with God's word. But many times it's our planning that's the problem. He edits our plans or our timing in order to help us realize the vision that he has given us.

Working Together

In **2:12-15** Nehemiah inspects the walls of Jerusalem. He goes out at night on a donkey—that's the only animal they take, so presumably the others are walking (**v 12**). When they get to the Fountain Gate, his donkey can't fit through (**v 14**). So he goes through on foot, inspecting everything. He seeks to gain as much information as he can, so as to make good decisions about what he is observing.

Nehemiah has not yet talked to the officials, who are the representatives of Persia; nor to the Jews, who are the citizens of that area; nor the priests, who will play a major role in the life of the community; nor to the nobles, which refers probably to the elders or the heads of households (**v 16**). But now that he has inspected the walls, he is ready to call them together, share his vision, and unify those who are willing to work for God's mission.

In **verse 17**, Nehemiah says to all these people, "You see the trouble we are in."

He doesn't say, *Look at this mess. Look at your neighborhood. My goodness. Look at all the trash on the ground. You should be ashamed of yourselves.* No, he says, "You see the trouble we are in." He includes himself as one of the people. Nehemiah doesn't separate himself from the circumstances of the people he is ministering to but enters into their issues and includes his lot with theirs. He even includes himself in their suffering—saying that he wants to rebuild "that we may no longer suffer derision." Nehemiah identified with his people. He relocated among them to serve them. "I also persevered in the work on this wall," he reported later (5:16). He didn't just supervise. He worked along with all the rest. Nehemiah didn't go to do the work for the people.

> Nehemiah enters into the people's issues and includes his lot with theirs.

Nor did he go just to give advice or supervision. He went to do it with the people.

This kind of attitude may remind us of someone. Just as Nehemiah was in a high place at the right hand of his king, but came down to Jerusalem to help his people, so Jesus Christ, having been eternally at the right hand of God the Father, came down into our circumstances to save us—enduring the shame of the cross.

"He had to be made like his brothers [i.e., humans] in every respect, so that he might become a merciful and faithful high priest in the service of God, to make **propitiation** for the sins of the people. For because he himself has suffered when tempted, he is able to help those who are being tempted."

(Hebrews 2:17-18)

Jesus had contextual connectivity. He was "made like his brothers." He was not only authentically human but also specifically connected to the Jewish nation. He had relevance to the context he was working in. He also had spiritual connectivity: he is "a merciful and faithful high priest in the service of God." He didn't go out trying to minister to people without having a spiritual connection to God. It's obvious that he has this connection in his **deity**—he is God, so of course he is connected with God—but he also lived it out in his humanity. In the Gospels we consistently see him withdrawing to pray. Finally, he had empathetic connectivity. "He suffered when tempted." Jesus let our issues become his issues. But even in the midst of those issues, Jesus did not sin. That means that he could both speak with authentic experience and bring redemption.

In many ways the **ministry** in our churches should be like Jesus' ministry. We should be relevant, we should be rooted in relationship with God, and we should own the issues in the communities we seek to serve. We have our own issues, but we also have to help others. Each of us was put where we are in order to help and develop others, not to look down on them. We have to stop talking about "those people" and "them" and start saying "us" and "our." Just like Nehemiah.

On top of this, the ownership of the solution, as well as that of the problem, is mutual. Nehemiah doesn't say, *Let me build the walls for you.* He says, "Let us build." He seeks not to build for people but to build with people. He wants to unify them all in this common project.

This applies to us as we seek to build God's kingdom in our local communities. Nehemiah is speaking to those who are part of God's people, and calling them to build together. In the same way, this call, "Let us build," is a call on God's people today. We are called to build God's kingdom—together. That is why, if someone who has been coming to our church for a year tells me, "I like what you all are do- ing here," I think, "Why not 'we'?" It's us. It's we. If you're part of a church, you're part of the community mission of that church. There has to be community ownership of the call of God on your life.

In order to establish unity among the people, Nehemiah says, "I told them of the hand of my God that had been upon me for good" (**v 18**). "The hand of ... God" is a recognition that God is the one initiating his visionary activity among his people. God's hand on us is the means by which he removes obstacles or sustains us through obstacles or even uses and appoints obstacles, to bring about the ends he desires. By his hand he sustains his people and glorifies his name. The hand of God—the way in which God had already acted to help Nehemiah—was proof that God was concerned about his people's condition.

So they respond, "Let us rise up and build." As soon as they hear that God is with them, "they strengthened their hands for the good work"—that means they encourage themselves. All they needed was to see the hand of God, and now they are ready to join in. At this point they are probably singing, worshiping, raising their hands, prais- ing God. They're full of hope. They're unified.

But there's a "but" coming.

Answering Enemies

"But when Sanballat the Horonite and Tobiah the Ammonite
servant and Geshem the Arab heard of it, they jeered at us and
despised us." (**v 19**)

Things are looking too good for the Jewish people, as far as Sanballat
and his friends are concerned. So they are full of contempt and ready
to exert energy against them. They say, "What is this thing that you
are doing? Are you rebelling against the king?"

They are accusing Nehemiah and trying to scare him. "What is this
thing that you are doing?" is a question that has appeared in the Bible
before. It is never a neutral question: it implies that the person has
done something terrible.

When Adam and Eve sinned, God said, "What is this that you
have done?" (Genesis 3:13). When Abram lied about the identity of
his wife—potentially drawing others into sin—Pharaoh asked Abram
the same question (Genesis 12:18). Abimelech asked it when Isaac
did the same thing (Genesis 26:10). When Laban deceived Jacob and
made him marry Leah instead of Rachel, Jacob said, "What is this
you have done?" (Genesis 29:25). And in Judges 2:2, God rebuked
the idolatry of Israel by saying, "What is this you have done?" So
when Sanballat says this, he is coming against the character of the
people of God—implying that they have been deceitful or faithless.
He is accusing them.

But Nehemiah doesn't pull out the letter from the king again to
prove his innocence. He doesn't argue with them at all. Instead he
says: "The God of heaven will make us prosper" (Nehemiah **2:20**).
Nehemiah doesn't answer a fool according to his folly (Proverbs 26:4).
He doesn't start going over the law of the Persian Empire. He just says,
*God is going to make it happen. His people are going to stop merely
surviving and start thriving.*

"The God of heaven" is Nehemiah's announcement (just as in 1:5)
of the sovereignty of God over everything. It's a phrase that is worth

saying if you are ever accused or attacked. Remind yourself of who your God is before you respond.

Nehemiah is then very clear and direct with his opponents. He is not interested in trying to persuade them to join his mission. He bluntly tells them that they are in the wrong—saying, "You have no portion or right or claim in Jerusalem."

It's helpful to be clear and direct with people when they are actively opposed to God—but we should also be in prayer for them. The opportunity still remains, for those who are opposed to the mission of God's people and to God himself, to repent, to embrace Christ, and to trust in him for salvation.

Nehemiah not only counted the cost but took on the challenge. And so he got to see God work in ways he would never have thought of if he had remained in Susa. He went from cupbearer to community activist and city leader, and then to governor. For him, we see that rebuilding was about God's plan, not personal position. In the next chapter we will see the work actually begin.

Questions for reflection

1. What is God calling you to at the moment? How can you test that the calling is really from him?

2. How can you make sure that your ministry is relevant, rooted in relationship with God, and connected to his people?

3. What will it look like to own the issues being experienced by the people you serve?

3. THE REBUILDING BEGINS

God has been at work among his people. They now commit themselves in a unity to build. This is the focus of the next two chapters of Nehemiah.

The wall encircling the city was a sign of its internal stability—or lack of it. Jerusalem was socially, economically, and spiritually without structure and stability. The nation was in distress socially because of continual oppression by foreign neighbors (see Ezra 4:7-23). The nation was in distress economically because of the heavy tax burden placed on the remnant by the Persians (see Nehemiah 5:1-5). The nation was in distress spiritually because of its failure to fully separate from the foreign nations (see Ezra 9:10-14). The people of Judah needed to be rebuilt in every sense—and the physical rebuilding of the walls would symbolize the social, economic, and spiritual rebuilding of the people.

God's name isn't mentioned once in Nehemiah 3, but he is deeply involved with and connected to every single thing going on. What does it look like for the good hand of God to be at work? In this case, it looks like him appointing his people to be a part of his rebuilding initiative. We're going to see in this passage that God uses human hands to build—and not just human hands in general but yours too.

Servant Leadership

Nehemiah **3:1** sets the tone for the entire chapter: "Then Eliashib the high priest rose up with his brothers the priests, and they built the Sheep Gate." It is significant that the high priest is the first person mentioned among those helping to rebuild the wall. Nehemiah doesn't mention the merchants yet, or the politicians, or the regular laborers. He begins with the spiritual leaders, who set the tone for how the work was to be done.

This was the high priest—not just any priest. This was the guy who would go into the Most Holy Place in the temple every year on Yom Kippur, the **Day of Atonement**. He had a uniquely high role as the person responsible for representing the people before God. And he was the one who first put his hand to the plough.

Eliashib's "brothers," the other priests, joined him. These were the other spiritual leaders who were responsible for teaching and shepherding Judah, and for making sacrifices for people—the various offerings of peace and thanksgiving and the sin and guilt offerings. Even though that was a very dirty and bloody job, it was viewed as a beautiful and glorious job, because this was the primary way in which God's people in those days (before Jesus) related to the living God.

These priests are spiritual leaders, but they recognize that their spiritual leadership has a practical impact. They set the tone for the community. That in turn sets the tone for how rebuilding takes place—not just here but whenever and wherever God works. He rebuilds through servant leaders.

It is very important that we see leadership as servanthood. Leadership is taking the initiative for the benefit of others; you lead, but your motivation is to serve. That means no one should lead just by telling people what to do. We have to lead by example.

Perhaps the best example of this is found in John 13, when Jesus got down on his knees and washed his disciples' feet. We too must be willing to get down on our knees to serve—to get dirty, stay up late, and do the kinds of things that Jesus would have done. We need to be creative and think of ways that we can serve.

When a leader serves, it motivates the rest of the people to serve, too. God calls all of us to serve. In fact, he is calling us to be a whole community of servant leaders. How do I know that? Because 1 Peter 2:9 calls us "a royal priesthood." This means that the church is the servant leader of any community. We are all priests together. Our role is to serve the people around us, lead them to God, and bring restoration. It is no coincidence that Eliashib's name means "God restores" or "God leads back." Restoration is what God wants to do among and through his people.

The opposite of servant leadership is selfish leadership. Alexander Strauch describes the difference between the two in his book on biblical eldership:

> "One seeks control to control people. The other seeks to serve people. One promotes self, but the other prostrates him or herself. One seeks prestige and position, but the other lifts up the lowly and the despised." (*Biblical Eldership: An Urgent Call to Restore Biblical Church Leadership*, p 77)

In Nehemiah 2, Sanballat, Tobiah, and Geshem began to sneer at and despise the work of God. They hated Nehemiah because he sought the welfare of the people. In other words, they weren't servant leaders but selfish leaders. When someone begins doing things for the people among whom God has placed them, what will happen is that others—those who are concerned about their own position—will be full of hostility. They will try to find something wrong with what this person is doing because they want the position of a leader without the posture of a servant. But God is calling us to be a community of servants—not trying to get glory and honor but accepting whatever position he puts us in.

What Is Built Is God's

The first thing that Eliashib and the other priests do is to build the Sheep Gate. Then "They consecrated it and set its doors" (Nehemiah **3:1**). "Consecrate" means "set something aside for a unique task." In Hebrew it is related to the word "holy." They consecrated this gate as a unique gate—and we'll get to the significance of this gate later.

In consecrating this gate they are pointing, first, to the fact that this entire project is set aside as a unique task for God's sake and, second, to the fact that it belongs to God.

Those two things have to go together. When we revel in the uniqueness and specialness of something we're doing under God and through God, we are in danger of beginning to worship the thing that God is doing through us. Consecration is a way of saying not only that something is special but also that it belongs to God—which will lead us to honor and worship him, not the work itself.

To consecrate the gate, the priests would have smeared either oil or blood on it. The practice of anointing things with oil continues today in some parts of the church. I myself recently anointed my sons with oil while I prayed for protection for them. I smeared it on their foreheads, and later on in the day I could still smell the sandalwood when they came over to me. The scent reminded me of my prayer and of the fact that they belong to God. It was the same with the gate; whenever anyone saw the blood or smelled the oil, they would be reminded that this gate was special and that it was God's.

Jesus too enacted this **sanctifying**, consecrating ministry—though without the oil. In John 17, acting like a high priest before the living God on behalf of the people of God, he prays a consecrating prayer. He says that his followers are in the world (v 11) but not of the world (v 14). In other words, we are special. But we are also his: we have been given to the Son by the Father (v 2), and we have eternal life because we know him (v 3). Jesus then asks the Father to sanctify (or consecrate) his people in the truth (v 17). In other words, if we are in Christ, then you and I have been set apart as special instruments of God. And we must never forget what this consecrating idea means. When something is special,

> If we are in Christ, then we have been set apart as special. We belong to God.

that means you treat it rightly. And when something belongs to God, that means you worship him for providing it.

God Rebuilds through Unity

There are also regular people on this job—as we see in the long list of names in Nehemiah **3:2-32**. "The men of Jericho" (**v 2**) have no special distinction; they're just ordinary people who have come to help. Then there are business owners: the perfumers (**v 8**), who are makers and sellers of perfumes; merchants (**v 32**)—people who sell all types of produce; and goldsmiths (**v 8**). I guess all these are there to restore the economy, but they are also there on the wall. There are families: brothers building together (**v 3, 18**) and daughters building with their father (**v 12**). Finally there are the politicians, the rulers of various districts (**v 9, 12, 14-19**), who are there to restore structure and social order to the community.

Why in the world would these people go to a broken-down, trash-ridden, dirty city to establish businesses, set up their families, and help organize the community? It is because they know the Lord. They have been transformed by a Yahweh-centered view of life. Their priorities for their lives—including their entrepreneurial practices, their choice of where to live, and their decision to commit to a particular people—reflected their faith.

Can you imagine a building project in your town in which the priests and pastors work beside the business owners, who work beside the teenagers, who work beside the mayor? That is what's happening in the passage. People from all walks of life were working together to rebuild the city so that God's people would be in a position to show him off.

Nobody was saying, "I really want to live in Jerusalem." But they were called; they knew where God had sent them. They saw redemption beyond the ruins.

The church today needs politicians. We need builders. We need businessmen and women. We need people who say, "We don't have enough supermarkets / coffee shops / thrift stores around here," and open one. We need people who actively seek the peace of their community. In other words, we need to become not just receivers but active workers for the Lord. There are ruins everywhere which God wants to rebuild through our hands.

This is a biblical issue, not just social service by itself. The gospel sets the tone for all the rebuilding and restoring we do. Isaiah 58:12 says, "Your ancient ruins shall be rebuilt; you shall raise up the foundations of many generations; you shall be called the repairer of the breach, the restorer of streets to dwell in." This isn't just talking about a city: it involves "the foundations of many generations." In other words, it has to do with people—people being restored by God. When God promises the restoration of streets, he is promising the transformation of people. And this can be done first and foremost through the message of Jesus Christ, who sent us out to build his church by making disciples of all nations (Matthew 28:18).

In this milieu of preparing, repairing and equipping, God has specifically recognized and called certain people to be the emerging pastor-teachers, evangelists, church planters and preachers of the word (Ephesians 4:11). Christ calls the people he places in these roles to prepare the church for service, unity and growth (Ephesians 4:12-13). The process takes time (2 Corinthians 3:18) but we can have faith that it will culminate in glory (Romans 8:29-30). The church in community is the best place for holistic community transformation (Matthew 16:13-19), as the strongholds of Satan are torn down, people come to Christ, and the brokenness in their lives is repaired. (You can read more about how this works in Harvie M. Conn and Manuel Ortiz's book, *Urban Ministry: The Kingdom, the City and the People of God*.)

Another important aspect of rebuilding is knowing what has to be done from scratch and what just needs to be strengthened.

Look at Nehemiah **3:3**: "The sons of Hassenaah built the Fish Gate." But then if you go to **verse 4**, it says, "And next to them Meremoth … repaired." It's the same all the way through the passage; sometimes it says "repair," sometimes "rebuild." In fact, "rebuild" is only used a few times, but "repair" goes all the way through.

Nehemiah recognized that there wasn't as much broken down as he thought. Instead of reinventing the wheel, he used what was already there. He went in where God was already at work. Likewise, as Christians, we need to begin to know what to start from scratch and what to repair and restore.

Back in **verse 1**, Eliashib and the other priests built the Sheep Gate. This gate was right at the northernmost tip of the city, which was the highest point in Jerusalem. This was where the sacrifices were brought into the city, because it was the closest gate to the temple in the north-eastern corner. That is probably where the gate derived its name: the sheep for sacrifice would come in that way. So it is significant that this was the first gate to be repaired. In Old Testament times, these sacrifices were the way for the people to come to God to ask for forgiveness and help. Without the sacrifices there could be no salvation; they pointed to Jesus' sacrifice on the cross, which finally secured salvation for sinners. Ultimately, then, this gate is a symbol of the cross.

It is also significant that the rebuilders did not consecrate the other gates. When the Sheep Gate had been consecrated, the whole wall was clean. That's the power of the gospel: once you are cleansed in Christ, you are entirely cleansed, not just partly (John 13:10).

There is another distinction between the Sheep Gate and the other gates that are rebuilt—the Fish Gate (Nehemiah **3:3**), the Gate of Yeshanah (**v 6**), the Valley Gate and the Dung Gate (**v 13-14**), and the Fountain Gate (**v 15**). In each of these verses, the builders "set its doors, its bolts, and its bars." But in **verse 1** it just says, "They consecrated it and set its doors." The Sheep Gate had no bolts and bars— no locks on it. Isn't that wonderful? The door to salvation is ever open to the sinner.

It is this that we need to place as central in our ministry. We may build buildings and open schools and organize food pantries and establish pregnancy-crisis centers and run cafes and start business-es and many other things. But if there is no gospel—if souls aren't transformed—we are only building a godless, Babylonian city. With the gospel, however, we are pointing to the ultimate Jerusalem that will come down from heaven, and to Jesus Christ himself.

So it is worth asking ourselves: Will I be a gospel witness where I live? Will I take responsibility to build the Sheep Gate for the people around me—to show them the way to salvation? Will I recognize that the gospel sets the tone? I pray that God will give us all grace to be builders for his name's sake.

Questions for reflection

1. If you are a leader, how can you make sure you keep having the attitude of a servant and avoid becoming selfish?

2. What difference will it make to your daily life to remember that you are consecrated or sanctified by Jesus?

3. What do you think might be the danger in focusing on social transformation without making the gospel central?

PART TWO

The people desired to see the city rebuilt in order that they might be set up to show off God's glory in every single area of their lives. They were excited about this. The Lord was stirring up their hearts, and everything was going well.

But whenever we sense God's presence and experience his provision, we have to take into account the fact that there is someone out there who doesn't like that at all. Every time we move forward in what God has called us to do, there is going to be opposition. For example, perhaps you have recently become a Christian, and life suddenly seems much harder. That's because now you're a target. God is conforming you to the image of Christ so that you reflect him on earth, and the enemy now turns his weapons on you.

The question is not whether or not God is going to use us. He will. Nor is it whether or not we are going to experience opposition. We will. The real question is: what are we going to do when opposition arises?

In Nehemiah 4, we continue to watch Nehemiah and all the people of Jerusalem. They have returned out of captivity and committed themselves to the work of the Lord. So far, everything has gone well. But in this chapter they meet with serious opposition. As we watch what happens, we can learn from Nehemiah how to continue to be productive for God's kingdom in the midst of opposition.

What Opposition Is About

The first thing we have to understand about opposition is that it comes to discourage kingdom productivity—that is, God's work in our lives.

Nehemiah **4:1** says, "Now when Sanballat heard that we were building the wall, he was angry and greatly enraged, and he jeered at the Jews." This must be intense hatred, because all these words are put together: Sanballat is not just "angry" but also "greatly enraged."

Listen to how deep it goes. Often we think that hate or opposition is pointed only toward us. But the questions that Sanballat begins to ask show where his anger really comes from. He is angry about God being glorified—about the honor God is getting out of someone else's life. His opposition is connected to the glory of God.

"What are these feeble Jews doing? Will they restore it for themselves? Will they sacrifice?" (**v 2**)

Sanballat's concern is that the Jews will succeed in rebuilding the city—resulting in God being glorified. He is also concerned that they're going to start making sacrifices. This is probably a reference to the traditional dedication ceremony: when the wall was completed, they would have a big party and honor God with sacrifices. It could also point to the Day of Atonement, when the people's sins would be dealt with. Sanballat doesn't want the people to honor God, and he doesn't want them to have a good relationship with God. That is what his opposition is truly about. It is the desire to see God get nothing.

Sanballat goes on: "Will they finish up in a day? Will they revive the stones out of the heaps of rubbish, and burned ones at that?" Some of the stones in the wall were broken and some were burned. Were they really going to use that material?

He doesn't understand how God works. We saw in Nehemiah 3 that the word "repair" is actually used more often than the word "rebuild." God likes to use broken and burnt stones that have been rejected and to repair them. This is most obviously true of Jesus—the stone that the builders rejected, which became the chief **cornerstone** for us (Matthew 21:42; Psalm 118:22). The one they threw away became the most important stabilizing factor in God's eternal plan. But in a different way, this is also true of us. God wants to use people out of their brokenness. He is near to the brokenhearted and close to those who are crushed in spirit (Psalm 34:18). He wants to use even the brokenness itself and the marks of the burning to honor his name. These things will show that it was God who revived and restored the person that was broken.

On and around South Street in Philadelphia, the street artist Isaiah Zagar has spent years making mosaic murals. He takes broken bottles, old plates, bicycle wheels, broken tiles, and lots of other things that most of us would just throw away. He puts it all together and creates art on ordinary walls. He has even created a mosaic garden. These murals have become a tourist attraction. They are beautiful. All of that trash has been brought together and revived, so that people who would have thrown it away now appreciate it. That is what God wants to do in our lives. He wants us to appreciate the value that is inherently in us through Jesus. He changes us so that we can continue to glorify him.

Next Sanballat's crony Tobiah speaks up, attacking the integrity of the work. He says it won't even stand. "If a fox goes up on it he will break down their stone wall!" (Nehemiah **4:3**) Of course, that's not true. When God rebuilds, he rebuilds quality stuff. But these haters don't like the fact that God is at work, and so they have to speak against the people.

Vent in Prayer

How will we respond when we meet opposition? We have to learn to do what Nehemiah does next. He goes straight into a prayer.

Sometimes we don't feel like praising God and giving him good words. We are hurt, and we can only be honest about that. These feelings may not seem very holy, but they can still be turned into prayer—which is exactly what Nehemiah does now.

"Hear, O our God, for we are despised. Turn back their taunt on their own heads and give them up to be plundered in a land where they are captives. Do not cover their guilt, and let not their sin be blotted out from your sight." (**v 4-5**)

Nehemiah is hurt. He is sick of these people and their insults. *Let them all go to hell:* that is the essence of what he's saying. That is what he asks God to do.

There are places in the Bible, including in the New Testament, which warn of the destruction of those who persecute believers and oppose God (2 Thessalonians 1:5-10; 2 Peter 2). But in these passages, it is God who is the Judge and Destroyer—not those who are being perse-cuted. So the lesson is that when we're opposed, sometimes we need to shut up and let God handle it. Be angry, be hurt, be upset—but bring those things to God rather than lashing out. If you don't bring your hurt to God, you just get angrier and angrier. It doesn't work. You need to move out of the way and let God deal with it.

> When we're opposed, we need to move out of the way and let God deal with it.

That is not to say that we should be utterly passive in the face of opposition or suffering. We'll see later in this chapter that Nehemiah takes the threat from Sanballat and Tobiah seriously and prepares to defend the city. But before he acts, he cries out to God.

Our benchmark for how to respond to opposition is Jesus Christ, who "also suffered for you, leaving you an example, so that you might follow in his steps. He committed no sin, neither was deceit found in his mouth. When he was reviled, he did not revile in return; when he suffered, he did not threaten, but continued entrusting himself to him who judges justly" (1 Peter 2:21-23). Jesus is the ultimate example of what it means to thrive in the face of opposition. He was opposed from the beginning of his ministry. He was kicked out of his hometown, in-terrogated by religious people, stalked by his enemies. Attempts were made to entrap him. He had a mole in his inner circle. He was aban-doned by those closest to him and framed for a crime he didn't commit. But throughout Jesus' experience of opposition, his character remained intact, and he continued doing what God had called him to do, unde-terred. He taught people, he made disciples, he healed sicknesses. He prayed for people who hated him. He entrusted himself to the one who judges justly. And on the cross he said, "Father, forgive them, for they know not what they do" (Luke 23:34).

If we are honest, by nature we are not like Nehemiah in this passage. We are like Sanballat and Tobiah and their friends. We were all God's opponents. We were those of whom it would have been right to say, "Let not their sin be blotted out from [God's] sight, for they have provoked [him] to anger." Yet God did choose to blot out our sin. We repented and put our faith in the one who dragged his cross up that hill and took those nails; the one who prayed for our forgiveness and bore our sin; the one who rose again on the third day with all power in his hands.

Now Jesus calls us to pick up our cross daily and follow him. That means that every day is an opportunity to deny ourselves to serve others and to thrive by growing in godliness even in the midst of opposition. Every day is a chance to talk about the fact that the God who was opposed has shown us how to walk in health and strength and restoration—and how to honor him no matter what.

Stay Focused

What do they do next? "We built the wall" (Nehemiah **4:6**).

I like that. Sometimes we need to just ignore haters and keep doing what God called us to do. Whatever the last thing was that God revealed to you to do, do it. Don't try to come up with something new to do. Don't let opposition change what God told you to do. After all, there's no productivity in doing what God hasn't called us to do. That's why they keep their hands on the wall. They don't shut down in the midst of opposition. They keep building the wall, and soon half of it is finished, "for the people had a mind to work."

Unsurprisingly, though, the opposition doesn't end there. It intensifies.

"When Sanballat and Tobiah and the Arabs and the Ammonites and the Ashdodites heard that the repairing of the walls of

Jerusalem was going forward and that the breaches were beginning to be closed, they were very angry. And they all plotted
together." (**v 7-8**)

People who don't usually get together start meeting. Sanballat's
group, the Samaritans, are from the north; the Arabs are from the
south, the Ashdodites are from the west, and the Ammonites are from
the east. Between them they surround Jerusalem.

God allows us to be surrounded sometimes. When Paul says, "We
are afflicted in every way" (2 Corinthians 4:8), the word "afflicted"
can be translated "pressed in," as if by crowds. But he continues,
"but not crushed." There's a limitation on how much God will let you
be pressed by the affliction. Even so, sometimes God will allow the
furnace to be heated up ten times hotter on purpose. He allows the
opposition to intensify.

That's what's happening to Nehemiah. His opponents have gone
from jeering to plotting.

They are particularly bothered by "the breaches" in the wall being
closed. The word "closed" takes its root from a word that means the
healing of a cut or wound. The wall is being healed. And Sanballat
and his friends don't like that. They hate it when God heals things. So
they turn up the heat. And God, by his grace, allows this intensifica-
tion of difficulty, for his honor and his glory and his praise.

How will God's people respond now? With prayer again—and with
action. "We prayed to our God and set a guard as a protection against
them day and night" (Nehemiah **4:9**). They take sensible precautions
to make sure they can keep going. And they focus on God, their help
and their strength.

We have to put our minds on him. "[God] keep[s] him in perfect
peace whose mind is stayed on [him]" (Isaiah 26:3). Circumstances
can be a mess, but when your mind is on the Lord Almighty, he can
change you in the midst of the circumstances.

God is bigger than your opposition. God is bigger than your brokenness. God is bigger than your frustration. God is bigger than your past.

God is bigger than your pain. God is bigger than your hurt. God is bigger than death. God is bigger than people who talked about you. God is bigger than the people who wrote you off. God is bigger than your loss. God is bigger than your sickness. God is bigger than you. So stay focused on him.

Questions for reflection

1. How do you respond to the idea that when we face opposition, it's really opposition against God?

2. How do you generally respond to hostility? Is there anything you would like to do differently?

3. How does this passage help you to understand what is happening when things go wrong?

4. DEFENSE AND DEVELOPMENT

At this point in the story, strength has begun to fail (**4:10**). It isn't that God's people are getting weak physically. They are getting sick and tired of the opposition, and they are becoming weakened in their hearts. "By ourselves we will not be able to rebuild the wall," they are saying to one another. They've been paying too much attention to the words of Sanballat and his cronies!

Today we would call Sanballat a "troll." An internet troll is someone who makes intentionally inflammatory, rude, or upsetting statements online to elicit strong emotional responses in people or to steer conversations off-topic. Most trolls do this simply for their own amusement, but some are pushing a specific political agenda. Sanballat was the second type. He wants to do harm—in his case, harm both to Nehemiah and to the mission of God. He was more than an emotional threat; he was a spiritual threat.

When this type of threat appears, the people of God have to decide in their own hearts: is it worth it to continue? Sanballat and God's other enemies have been trying to get the people of God to fear them. They are planning to come and fight against Jerusalem. And the people are scared. Will they keep going?

Yes. Nehemiah finds out and tells everybody to get on the wall. He lines them up "with their swords, their spears, and their bows" (**v 13**). Then he reminds them that they serve the great and awesome God. And he calls on them to contend while they build.

Building like this is a balance between defense and development.

We have to recognize that while we build in the Lord's strength, we are also going to be fighting. There is nothing worthwhile that God has called us to build that we won't have to fight for while we build it. We need to be people who stand face to face before whatever is in front of us and say, "God, this is a battle that you've put me in. God, I want to make sure that I stand for you. I'm going to put on my divine gloves, and I'm going to make sure that I'm ready for the battle."

Fighting is part of being a Christian. As we build, we have to learn how to fight.

Contending for God's Glory

In **verse 14** Nehemiah gives a short speech to the people to encourage them to contend for what they are building. He doesn't simply tell them to muster up their energy in the flesh. He tells them first of all, *I want you to look at who God is.* When they look at who God is, then they will be ready to fight.

"Do not be afraid," Nehemiah tells the people. "Remember the Lord."

I imagine at this point that everyone suddenly puts their head up. *Remember the Lord?* They've been focusing on their own weakness, their own fears, their own limitations—but Nehemiah doesn't talk about any of that. He says, "Remember the Lord…" Then he adds: "…who is great and awesome."

We sometimes have a picture of God as an emasculated old man with a long beard, shriveled up, with varicose veins, sitting far away on a throne in eternity. But this God that Nehemiah is preaching is the great and awesome God who dwells in unapproachable light (1 Timothy 6:16). No sinful human can just come up into the presence of the awesome God. He is the one who spoke in the darkness and called light into existence; sin cannot stand in his presence. Everything has to obey him. This is the God whom Nehemiah is talking about: a fire-and-brimstone God. At the same time this God is more loving than it is even possible to imagine—and he fights for his people. This is the God they need to remember.

Only after they have remembered this God does Nehemiah say, "Fight."

In the New Testament, terms related to physical fighting are used to describe the spiritual battle we face. When Paul says, "I have fought the good fight," he means he has "kept the faith"—he has persevered (2 Timothy 4:7). Nehemiah's literal call to fight may at first seem far removed from this type of spiritual fighting. But bear in mind that Paul's spiritual fight has not just been about himself. He has not "fought" just in the sense of maintaining his own private belief in God. He has fought for other people. He has endured hardship upon hardship in order to bring the gospel to communities across the Mediterranean and to encourage and build up his fellow believers.

What Nehemiah says to the people shows that his heart is the same as Paul's. He says, *Fight for your brothers. Fight for your sons. Fight for your daughters. Fight for your wives. Fight for your homes.* These fighters are not just saving their own skins. They're fighting for others.

Why? Because that is how God displays his glory. God helps the world to know how great he is through his people, who are transformed through his gospel. We fight for people—our brothers, our families, and our homes—because we are fighting to make God's glory known.

Fight for Your Brothers

"Brothers" doesn't just mean "family members." In Jewish culture, "brothers" was a broader term than that. It meant people from the same country or ethnicity as you. It could also include converts to Judaism. So the people on the wall of Jerusalem were fighting for one another whether they were biologically related or not.

In the New Testament the word "brothers" is used slightly differently again, this time to refer to other Christians—because we've all been saved into the same family of God. Nigerian, Ghanaian, Latino, Caribbean, Italian, Irish, Polish, British, Chinese, Indian... God places together people from all these backgrounds and more. We have become brothers and sisters. The church of Christ has been multicultural throughout history, as church historian Vince Bantu points out:

> "Many contemporary missiologists and church historians would have us believe that Christianity came into Africa and Asia from Europe when the reality is quite the opposite in several significant respects. Christianity is not becoming a global religion; it has always been a global religion."
>
> (*A Multitude of All Peoples*, p 2)

It can be easy to forget this when many of us spend most of our time with Christians from the same background as ourselves. But we need to look up and out. We should be contending for one another: praying and standing up for those who are our brothers and sisters in Christ in other countries and other communities. We should fight for one another as brothers and sisters even when we come from communities or nations which are hostile to one another.

But it is also right to have a particular burden for those who are our countrymen in a non-spiritual sense. As we see the needs and struggles of others in our families, in our nation, and in our world, we can let theology inform our sociology. Being spiritually destitute has social ramifications: where people are cut off from God, we will see oppression, violence, gossip, lies, foolishness. We will see damaging relationships and broken societies. As those who believe in the God who hates sin and promises restoration, we should be concerned about the people who are worst off in our countries and in our neighborhoods. We should "fight for [our] brothers."

This means seeking to share the gospel, most importantly. But it also means asking ourselves: How can we care for these people in a way that will develop common ground and form trusting relationships between us? How can we build bridges to them socially which will enable us to engage with them spiritually with Jesus, the truth?

Titus 3:14 says, "Let our people learn to devote themselves to good works so as to help cases of urgent need, and not be unfruitful." God has called his people to meet pressing needs—that's what being fruitful looks like. Caring for people socially is part of the mission he has called us to. It is to his glory.

Fight for Your Families

What about our sons, our daughters, and our wives? What might it look like to fight for them?

Fighting for your children means fighting to ensure that they can't remember a day when Jesus wasn't being invested into their souls. It means developing a family worship time in which you point the whole household heavenward. It means creating memories for your children of precious worship and times of prayer; it means teaching them the Bible. It means talking to them about what it means to follow Christ.

Sons often want to boast in their fathers and daughters in their moms; but fighting for them for God's glory means that you will not allow them to idolize you. You will point them to Jesus so that they won't center their identity on you. In fact, you'll begin admitting to your children how trifling you are so that they cannot idolize you but only Jesus Christ, who has forgiven you and is restoring you. They will know how to repent of sin because they have seen repentance modeled by Daddy and Mommy.

Fight for your wives—that might mean fighting for your marriage. There are difficult times in every marriage in which you don't feel like you love each other and you want to be distant from one another. Those times are when you need to fight. Again, this cannot be done without first remembering the Lord. You fight by letting the cross close the distance between you. Don't just be in close proximity to one another and get on each other's nerves. Get in close proximity to God. When you come into God's presence in prayer, you start to see your deficiencies, and you recognize that God should have distanced himself from you a long time ago. And then you will say, "If God can give me his presence like this, why can't I give my spouse my presence?"

In Everything, Fight for Christ

Finally, we are to fight for our homes. In the context of the passage, that means fighting to represent God. They weren't just fighting to make sure their houses weren't knocked over. They were fighting for Jerusalem. "Homes" meant a tabernacling place for the glory of God (see pages 11-13 and 15-16).

That's a helpful corrective to us as we fight for our brothers and families. Because the thing we are ultimately fighting for is God's glory in our lives, we must not idolize any of these other things. We fight for our brothers and our children and our wives—but all of them come second to Christ.

> We fight for our brothers, our children, our wives—but all of them come second to Christ.

Jesus himself challenges us on those very things in Luke 18:29-30. "Truly, I say to you, there is no one who has left house or wife or brothers or parents or children, for the sake of the kingdom of God, who will not receive many more times in this time, and in the age to come eternal life." In other words, God calls us to put our houses and our families and all the things we hold most precious on an altar to him; to say, "They belong to you, God"; to be ready to give them up.

And Jesus says that if we give up our lives for his kingdom, he'll give them back to us better than the way we presented them to him. Just as the tools to build a car in my hands would make a mess, but the tools to build a car in a mechanic's hands will make a sellable car—and just as the tools for building a wall in my hands would result in a mess, but the tools to build a wall in the hands of a bricklayer will result in a level wall—so too my life in my hands is nothing much, but in Jesus' hands, it can be used for God's glory.

We need to submit and release everything in our lives to Jesus—not giving in to fear, nor putting other things in God's place, but fighting for his glory. "Remember the Lord, who is great and awesome." There is no one more powerful than him, and there is no one who loves us more than he does. So let's find our purpose in God—not in work, not in prestige, not in music, not in money, not in our families in themselves, but first and foremost in God, the King of kings and the Lord of lords. Then let's fight for those other things wherever they are an opportunity to give him glory.

Accept Responsibility

In Luke 4:16-21, Jesus goes to the **synagogue**, unrolls the scroll of Isaiah, and reads out a passage from Isaiah 61: "The Spirit of the Lord is upon me, because he has anointed me to proclaim good news to the poor. He has sent me to proclaim liberty to the captives and recovering of sight to the blind, to set at liberty those who are oppressed, to proclaim the year of the Lord's favor." The Lord Jesus Christ was sent with a purpose, and he saw that purpose in the Scriptures. He was willing to take responsibility to do what the Father had sent him for—which included not only the saving of sinners but the work of healing, restoring, teaching, and serving which he did throughout his life and now still does through the Holy Spirit. He was willing to fight to rebuild those who needed rebuilding.

We, too, need to accept responsibility for the work God has given us to do. We need to say to ourselves, "Do not be afraid. Remember the Lord, who is great and awesome, and fight."

Questions for reflection

1. How does this chapter challenge your understanding of what it means to fight for faith?

2. Practically, what will it look like for you to fight for the glory of Christ in your family, in your church, and in your community?

3. Why is it so important to keep fixing our eyes on Christ as we fight for him and for others?

PART TWO

In Nehemiah **4:15** Nehemiah tells us what happened next. "Our enemies heard that it was known to us and that God had frustrated their plan."

The remainder of chapter 4 gives us the details of the actions Nehemiah took to make the builders ready to fight. But God had already frustrated their enemies' plans. Their schemes would no longer work. Why? Because the people had stopped walking in fear and started walking in faith again. They had remembered the Lord. They were ready to fight.

When we're fearful of something that is not God, it becomes an idol. We worship it by fearing it—it takes a place in our minds and our hearts that is higher than God's. This is what the enemy of the glory of God wants. He will seek to put our faith in captivity and fill us with fear instead.

These enemies surrounded Jerusalem. They could have destroyed God's people. But their plans were frustrated—not because God's people were strong, not because they were powerful, but because they stood in awe of the reality of who God was and because that motivated them to fight. God himself was responsible for this. He restored his people's faith through Nehemiah. God is the one who frustrated his enemies' plans.

Now they were ready both to keep on building and to contend for God's glory. It is the combination of both these that we see in this last section of Nehemiah 4.

One Work, Many Assignments

So what do they do? "We all returned to the wall, each to his work" (**v 15**). They keep on with their original task.

A few verses later, in **verse 17**, it's called "the work." When God frustrates the plan of the enemy, the people return not to *their* work but to *the* work.

What God does on earth for his glory doesn't belong to anybody but him. Because of that, it's called "the work." Not "your work." God isn't going to support *your* work unless you're supporting *the* work. If we try to build another work, we're building something else, not the work; which means we're now contending against God instead of beside him. We need to recognize that there's only one work. That's just the way it works!

We may have a church here, we may have a person there, but there is only one work of God on our planet. The worldwide church is God's work on the earth: a magnification of his mission to reach lost people and to lift them up. The church doesn't belong to any pastor or any bishop. It doesn't belong to any of us. It belongs to God. We are simply rallying around him and joining him. It's only one work.

But within the big work of God, everybody has an assignment. "We all returned … each to his work." Each person is a small part of the grand scheme.

There's a gas station near where I live which has four or five little garage doors. One says, "Alignment." One says, "Oil Change." Another says, "Brakes." These are different garages that have different assignments within the gas station. Every believer is like one of those garages. 1 Corinthians 12:4-7 tells us, "There are varieties of gifts, but the same Spirit; and there are varieties of service, but the same Lord; and there are varieties of activities, but it is the same God who empowers them all in everyone. To each is given the manifestation of the Spirit for the common good." Even though there's a different name on each person's task, all of us who are in

> There's a different name on each person's task, but in Christ we're all part of one work.

Christ are part of one work, and that's the building of the kingdom of Christ.

Here's how we see this worked out very practically in Nehemiah's plans. "Half of my servants worked on construction, and half held the spears, shields, bows, and coats of mail" (Nehemiah **4:16**). These are two different assignments: some people build; some people are ready to fight. Then there are those who lead, who are standing behind them, presumably to direct the work.

Contending While Building

Can you imagine people working on a house with a paint roller in one hand and an AR-15 in the other? And others walking the perimeter as guards while the home is being built? That's the picture here. Nehemiah has set them up to be prepared for attack, without being distracted from what they were supposed to do. They take the enemy's threats seriously but don't let them consume them to the point of stagnation. They are still prioritizing the building of the wall, even as they get ready to fight to defend it. The work includes both tasks. Development and defense are supposed to happen at the same time when you're honoring God.

That is why the people who carried burdens (presumably building tools and materials) were "loaded in such a way that each labored on the work with one hand and held his weapon with the other" (v **17**). Likewise, each of the builders "had his sword strapped at his side while he built" (**v 18**).

Recently, I received tons of messages online from black identity groups and right-wing **evangelicals**. These groups were messaging me for differing reasons. The right-wing evangelicals didn't like the fact that I was speaking out on racial injustice, and the black mystery cult members were angry because I was calling them out on how they were spreading false and misinformed narratives about Christianity. As the attacks came, I had to be very careful of getting sucked in. I defended my position where needed, for clarity for the people that follow our ministry. But I had to keep the work of ministry in our lo-cal community going, and responding to absolutely everything could have been a massive distraction. I had to gauge how to balance the construction and contending.

The church has always had to balance this. Jude verse 3 points to the fact that the church had to defend and build at the same time: "Although I was very eager to write to you about our common salva-tion, I found it necessary to write appealing to you to contend for the faith." Jude had to focus on defense on this occasion. Elsewhere the two were to be done simultaneously. Paul states how his ministry commendation is affirmed "with the weapons of righteousness for the right hand and for the left" (2 Corinthians 6:7). The NLT translates it, "We use the weapons of righteousness in the right hand for attack and the left hand for defense." At different times and in different ways, we are all called to do both.

Rallying Points

The final role listed in these verses is that of the man who sounded the trumpet, who stayed beside Nehemiah (Nehemiah **4:18**). The trumpet back then would have been a crooked ram's horn, which the trum-peter would blow into as a battle cry. Nehemiah told the people that when the trumpeter blew into the ram's horn, it meant that he want-ed them all to gather in one place (**v 19-20**). They needed the sound of the trumpet to rally them because they were far apart on the wall.

When they came together at the rallying point, they would be given instructions so that when they were scattered back out into battle, they would know what they were actually supposed to do. The function of the trumpet was to make sure that everyone was on the same page.

That points to a beautiful principle in the theology of mission: scat-tering and gathering. When God scatters us out into the work that he's called us to in the world, we are to be working, and working hard;

but there also has to be a time of rallying together. We need to come together and make sure we are on the same page.

The first thing we rally around is the triune God. If we're not on the same page about who God is, we can't rally together. He is the one that drafted us. The Father chooses, the Son saves, and the Spirit seals (Ephesians 1:1-14).

The second rallying point is the Bible. We can say we believe in the same God, but we don't really unless we agree on how he has spoken and how he has revealed himself. So the Bible is where we rally. That means that we don't make stuff up—saying, "God told me this" when it's not in line with God's word. We ask, "What does the Bible say?" And it means having a biblical worldview. We don't meet around our opinions; we let the Bible transform our opinions.

Prayer is the third rallying point. We need to have a prayer life, not just when we're in trouble but all the time. We need an ongoing dialogue with God so that when trouble happens, we're not trying to conjure a fellowship that we never had before—just as Nehemiah's men stood ready to fight before anyone had attacked.

Acts 2:42-47 is a wonderful description of the way the early church gathered together.

"And they devoted themselves to the apostles' teaching and the fellowship, to the breaking of bread and the prayers. And awe came upon every soul, and many wonders and signs were being done through the apostles. And all who believed were together and had all things in common. And they were selling their possessions and belongings and distributing the proceeds to all, as any had need. And day by day, attending the temple together and breaking bread in their homes, they received their food with glad and generous hearts, praising God and having favor with all the people. And the Lord added to their number day by day those who were being saved."

They were Christ-centric—devoting themselves to "the breaking of bread" and to the teaching about Jesus. Without Christ, we can do nothing. "He is before all things, and in him all things hold to-gether" (Colossians 1:17). God is reconciling the world to himself through Jesus Christ. Jesus has to be central.

They were committed: not just hearing the word but obeying what they heard. They came together, put the one who is perfect at the center, and listened to him. They were a community: coming together to love each other, admitting their mess and their need for help, and sharing what they had.

Missiologist Lois Barrett explores what this looked like economically:

"It is likely that the early church in Jerusalem was adapting **Jubilee law** to an urban setting when it instituted the practice of sharing all goods in common (Acts 2:44-45; 4:32-35). Even where the early church did not hold all goods together, it still practiced economic sharing. Paul collected money from the church in Macedonia for the needs of the church in Jerusalem. In numerous places, the Epistles urge Christians to share with the needy (e.g., Romans 12:13; Ephesians 4:28). Indeed, they even suggest that it is impossible for God's love to be in anyone who has the world's goods, sees a brother or sister in need, and yet refuses to help (1 John 3:17)."

(in Darrell L. Guder, *Missional Church*, p 121-122)

At the same time, this was not an inward-looking, ingrown communi-ty where you were always with other Christians but never touched the lost. This was a community that saw conversions: people going from spiritual death to spiritual life. "The Lord added to their number day by day those who were being saved." In other words, the people of God got together with purpose and went out with purpose. They had lives that were gathered enough to develop and support one another, but scattered enough to go into the world and engage lost people.

This is what our churches should be like today. We gather together to be built up around Christ, and we scatter into the world to fight for him. Sunday mornings are like the trumpet call of Nehemiah's trum-peter: calling us together to be resourced and to be reminded of the glorious gospel so that when we go out into the world again, we will cultivate a cross-centered life.

Jesus Has Won

This, then, is Nehemiah's plan for contending while building. He is not paralyzed by fear but makes wise plans to defend the city at the same time as pushing on with the rebuilding. We see the principle of combining defense with development.

But the most fundamental part of Nehemiah's plan is the last thing he says in Nehemiah **4:20**. "Our God will fight for us."

The people didn't just put on war clothes and strap swords to their sides. They understood that God was the one that actually did the fighting. Even when they threw out their arms to fight, it was really God's arm over theirs, cutting at things that they couldn't see. And, in fact, he had already frustrated their enemies' plans.

You may already think of life as a fight—full of struggle and pain and difficulty and danger. You may be used to fighting on your own. But when we're fighting for the cause of Christ, that makes the battle so much easier! We have nothing to worry about and nothing to be afraid of—because we're not fighting for victory. We're fighting from victory. Jesus has already won.

After all, the greatest place where we see the principle of defense and development played out is on the cross. Colossians 2:14-15 says, "The record of debt that stood against us with its legal demands ... he set aside, nailing it to the cross. He disarmed the rulers and authorities and put them to open shame by triumphing over them." In other words, the enemy had bullets, but Jesus Christ took the bullets out of the gun. The cross is a defensive weapon that has disarmed the evil one.

But the cross is also a tool of development. In Romans 1:15 Paul wrote to the Roman Christians, "I am eager to preach the gospel to you also who are in Rome" (Romans 1:15). Why does he say that he wants to preach the gospel to Christians? Because it's not only a defensive weapon. The gospel is not just something that saves unbelievers. It is also for us, to develop and rebuild us. It doesn't just save us but also continues to transform us; it keeps us safe and takes us to the new heavens and the new earth—to be with the one who died for us.

We must recognize that Nehemiah **4:19-20** ultimately points to Jesus. When Christ is the center of why we fight, then we are empowered with true weaponry. We can follow him in his work by contending while building. We can build and fight to the glory and honor of Jesus Christ.

Questions for reflection

1. What evidence can you see in your own church of how God calls people to many different assignments but all to one work?

2. How can you make the most of your church gatherings so that you are resourced and prepared for going out into the world?

3. Where do you see a need to balance defense with development or fighting with building? What will it look like to wisely combine both?

5. REBUILT THROUGH JUSTICE AND LOVE

We've seen God providing resources for the city to be rebuilt—and for the people themselves to be rebuilt. But then they started going through some difficult times. In chapter 4 the opposition came from outside, but now there are problems within Jerusalem itself.

In chapter 5 we will see the challenges surrounding justice. There was an economic crisis. The poor were short of food (Nehemiah **5:2**), and the landowners were compelled to mortgage their properties (**v 3**). Some were forced to borrow money at exorbitant rates because of oppressive taxation (**v 4**), and some were even forced to sell their children into slavery (**v 5**).

This chapter makes me think of some of the things that go on in our own societies. There is injustice, poverty, crime, economic oppression, inequality, and anger. There are people going through terrible challenges.

I'm not only talking about extreme violence. I'm talking about family issues, alcoholism, mental illness, debt: all the things that make people cry out in despair because they can see no way out. These things are not just social issues; they are gospel issues. As Christians we know that it is the gospel that transforms people. It transforms the inside of them in such a powerful way that it changes and challenges even the most difficult circumstance.

There's no issue anywhere that God cannot invade and transform through his power. In Nehemiah 5 we see God at work even in the midst of these difficult times. The people cry out, and they are rebuilt through justice and love.

The Cries of the Broken

The first thing we must do if we are to see the gospel rebuild people is to listen to their cries.

"Now there arose a great outcry of the people." (**v 1**)

This idea of outcry is used throughout Scripture. It means people who are dealing with challenges and difficulty crying out because they can't take it anymore. It's the yell for help from someone's heart. The same word was used of Israel when they were in slavery in Egypt crying out to God (Exodus 3:7, 9). A strong outcry frequently indicates that righteousness and justice are absent, so the gravity of the situation is underscored in that term.

What's notable here is that we're told that the wives were joining in. Usually in that culture the men were the ones to speak out, but here the situation had got so bad that absolutely everybody was talking about it.

They are crying out "against their Jewish brothers" (Nehemiah **5:1**): that is, against their own people. Significantly, the people's complaints were not lodged against the foreign authorities but against their own fellow countrymen.

Why were they crying out? **Verse 2** tells us: "For there were those who said, 'With our sons and daughters, we are many.'" That is, the city had become overcrowded. There were more people in the city than resources for each family. So the people were saying, "Let us get grain, that we may eat and keep alive.'" There was a desperation within the city of Jerusalem. They were hungry.

Biblically, famines were often induced by God because of judgment. From Egypt to Judges and Ruth, to the time of Elijah, we see this over and over. But this famine in Nehemiah isn't a famine of judgment. It has happened simply because of overcrowding; there are more people and very few resources.

Commentator H.G.M. Williamson notes, "Since Nehemiah had forbidden the men to return home from Jerusalem while the wall was being built, the farms may have been severely understaffed during the crucial period of ingathering" (*Ezra, Nehemiah*, p 236). That is to say, human resources were already squeezed because of the necessity of defending the city. There weren't enough men to staff the farms. That was why there was not enough food to go around. And certain people were taking advantage of this situation to exploit their poorer brethren. In the midst of this shortage, people are willing to do whatever they have to do to make sure that they survive.

Next it says there are those who are mortgaging their fields (**v 3**). In order to eat, they're mortgaging their houses, their fields, their vineyards. That means they're getting rid of businesses, too—all to get grain because of the famine, and because they have committed themselves to building the wall.

Then taxes increase (**v 4**): "And there were those who said, 'We have borrowed money for the king's tax on our fields and our vineyards.'" Not only are they mortgaging their homes and businesses to get food; they're also doing so in order to pay taxes. So now they're in debt.

What happens next is crazy. What happened in this culture when you couldn't pay your bills? You used your possessions as collateral. But you used more than just fields, more than just vineyards and houses; you also used children. You put your children into slavery if you couldn't pay your debts. And this is what the people in Jerusalem were doing (**v 5**).

This slavery was not like the **chattel slavery** of black people in America, where slaves were stripped of their identity and their dignity in every possible way. But it was still not good. It meant heavy indentured servitude: you were like a servant, but you served without wages until you had paid your debt or someone else paid it for you.

"It is not in our power to help it," say their parents (**v 5**); they have nothing left to pay their creditors with. We see in **verse 7** that these parents not only have to pay back what they have mortgaged, but they have to pay it with interest. The people who are loaning them the money know they can't ever pay it back in full. Which would make this much more like chattel slavery.

And it isn't **heathens** who are doing this to the poor. It is the so-called religious people: the "Jewish brothers" (**v 1**). These are the ones who are taking advantage of the resource shortage by oppressing those who are poor.

What a major parallel to slavery and oppression in the United States. This chapter alone is rich with principles for biblical application to racial injustice and other systemic injustices. It is immensely clear that these "Jewish brothers" walked in some type of blindness in order to justify their treatment of their Jewish brethren. We see the same blindness today in the systemic injustice that is found in **redlining**, school-to-prison pipelines, abortion rates, and police brutality. Much of what we are dealing with today is connected to a long history of hypocrisy and oppression. By contrast, it is beyond commendable that Nehemiah dealt with the hypocrisy of his brethren early and didn't let it fester and go too far. He heard the cry for justice, and he acted on it.

> Nehemiah heard the cry for justice, and he acted on it.

Nehemiah Acts

Nehemiah gets ticked off when he hears the people's cries. He is "very angry" (**v 6**). But he doesn't just sympathize with their complaints. He acts. He brings two legal charges against the officials and the well-to-do people who have been oppressing the poor.

First, in **verse 7**, "You are exacting interest, each from his brother." It was ok in Jewish law to loan a brother or sister money. It was lawful to loan money. But you were supposed to loan with no interest (Deuteronomy 23 v 19), whereas these people are loaning on top of loans. They are acting against God's law.

Second, "we, as far as we are able, have brought back our Jewish brothers who have been sold to the nations, but you even sell your brothers that they may be sold to us!" (Nehemiah **5:8**). Some of the people are able to be in Jerusalem only because Nehemiah has bought their freedom from foreign masters. But now the nobles and officials are forcing into slavery the very people they should be welcoming as their brothers. They are seeing them as people to exploit, rather than as fellow members of the people of God. Sound familiar?

After Nehemiah outlines these charges, the men he is accusing are silent (**v 8**). They cannot find a word to say to defend themselves.

What Injustice Really Is

In **verse 9** Nehemiah identifies the root of the injustice these men are perpetrating. "The thing that you are doing is not good. Ought you not to walk in the fear of God?"

Walking in the fear of God means taking God seriously. And God is a just God. He doesn't do right merely because he is choosing to. He does it out of the nature of who he is. God is right and does right, always. It is because God is just that we can know what justice is and act with justice ourselves. Injustice, therefore, is not simply the implication of a legal system—something humans have decided is wrong; it is something that is contrary to God's nature.

It is because the nobles and officials are not walking in the fear of God that they are acting unjustly. If we know God, if we are awestruck by him, it should make us reach out in our heart and in our actions to the needs of somebody else, to help them and never to exploit them.

The fear of God asks, "What does God feel about this situation? How does the gospel speak to this situation? Holy Spirit, how can you show up to bring transformation in this situation?"

Too often unbelievers are able to think that Christians come to church on a Sunday, talk about stuff with no relevance to real life and real difficulties, and then retreat back to their own comfortable homes. What we should be doing as churches is developing common ground with our neighbors—with the hurting, with the lost—so that we can share Jesus with them and show that the gospel is relevant to them.

In the 2009 film *Precious*, the title character is a teenager living in poverty and pregnant with her second child due to being raped by her own mostly absent father. In one scene she tells her counselor, "You can't handle all this." She's saying, *My stuff is so wrecked. You don't want to come into my life. What have you got that can change my world?* That's what people are going to say to us, too. Will we hear their voices? Will we cry with them? And then, will we say, "Yes, I do have something that can bring change"?

Ultimate Justice

In the end, of course, the answer to injustice is Jesus.

He came "to proclaim good news to the poor ... to proclaim the year of the Lord's favor" (Luke 4:18-19). This was Jesus' mission statement: he came to preach the good news to those who were most broken. This good news was only good news because Jesus came not only in word but also in deed. The good news he was proclaiming was the good news of the cross.

We are all like the oppressive nobles and officials in Nehemiah 5: we don't fear God as we should, and we don't act rightly. We deserve punishment. However, God is a God of love and of grace, and he wanted to save us. And so Jesus Christ came, without sin, to die on the cross and take the punishment on behalf of all of us. Because he took and was able to withstand the full blow of God's **wrath**, now God can apply grace and mercy and love to those of us who trust in him, without us dying the way Jesus did. We can gain the Holy Spirit and be regenerated from the inside out.

This was why Jesus said he came "to proclaim the year of the Lord's favor." He's speaking about the year of jubilee. This does not mean what the people on TV say it does: "It's the year of jubilee and everybody must give so they can get more money. Everybody's debt is going to be released." No, God's favor runs much deeper than financial gain. Jesus was dealing with the same deep issues of injustice and pain which the people in Jerusalem had experienced—and more. He came to put an end to injustice forever.

He said, "Come to me, all who labor and are heavy laden, and I will give you rest. Take my yoke upon you, and learn from me, for I am gentle and lowly in heart, and you will find rest for your souls" (Matthew 11:28-29). The favor Jesus came to proclaim is about justice and freedom. It is about gaining forgiveness for sin, transformation inside out, and life for eternity.

Repentance

Nehemiah models something of what Jesus would come to bring in the way that he deals with the oppressive nobles and officials.

He says, "Let us abandon this exacting of interest" (Nehemiah **5:10**). Basically, *Let us repent of this.* The oppressors are to return everything they have been given as collateral for debt, as well as all the interest they have been paid (**v 11**). In other words, all the people's debts are to be cleared.

Nehemiah guarantees justice and reparation for the poverty-stricken inhabitants of Jerusalem. But at the same time, instead of punishing the oppressors, Nehemiah gives them a second chance: a chance to make things right—not just to stop the oppression but to reverse it. This was the ultimate sign of repentance.

It seems as if urban renewal wasn't the only thing that Jerusalem needed. The walls being repaired was only a sign of the relational and heart repair that was needed. Repairing hearts is the most critical requirement for long-term and long-lasting change to take place. Nehemiah knew this, so he made them swear that they would do as he said (**v 12**).

This could be no empty promise: it came with a threat. "I also shook out the fold of my garment and said, 'So may God shake out every man from his house and from his labor who does not keep this promise'" (**v 13**). Nehemiah was giving them an ultimatum. They would have a second chance, but ultimately, if they went back to their sinful ways, they would run out of chances. God's grace is abundant, but we do have to take our sin seriously and turn to him in genuine repentance.

Questions for reflection

1. What social or economic injustices do you see around you? How can you make sure you listen to the cries of the broken?

2. How can we make sure we keep the gospel central as we respond practically to injustices?

3. What injustices have you yourself participated in? Is there anything you need to repent of?

PART TWO

In **verses 14-19** we learn that Nehemiah has taken upon himself the expense and pain of looking after the people in the city of Jerusalem. In a way, the punishment for injustice has been laid on him, because he has made sacrifices for them. He has surrendered his rights for them.

Surrendering rights is the willingness to forego God-given freedoms that are not absolutely necessary, in order to benefit others instead of yourself and bring glory to God. Let me give you an example. When I was a very little boy, my mother used to wake up at four thirty or five o'clock in the morning. She'd make my lunch and iron my clothes, and then be out to work by five thirty or six. She'd then work all day, sometimes until ten o'clock at night, earning money to look after me and make sure that I could go to a school in another neighborhood instead of the hard neighborhood we lived in. When I was young, I didn't really appreciate this, but looking back I realize how much she sacrificed for my sake.

Nehemiah is a little like that. He makes sacrifices for the sake of the people and the wall-building project. He is looking for ways to make sure the mission of God gets done, without that being at the expense of the people of God.

Nehemiah's Rights

As governor of Judah, appointed by Artaxerxes, the king of Persia, Nehemiah had the right to add his own tax onto the king's taxes. This was the right of every Persian governor (see Victor Harold Matthews, Mark W. Chavalas, and John H. Walton, *The IVP Bible Background Commentary*, on this verse). It was to pay his salary and buy his food. Nehemiah also had an entourage of about 150 men (**v 17**). Most governors would raise the salaries of these employees through this same tax. They wouldn't just raise the money they strictly needed: they would tax people hard so that they themselves could eat luxuriously and employ a lot of servants. This means that the people had been used to leadership that brutally took from them rather than looking out for their good: governors who had "lorded it over" them (**v 15**), using all the rights the king had given them for their own selfish purposes.

But Nehemiah and his entourage didn't eat the food allowance they were entitled to (**v 14**), and they didn't exact the heavy taxes the people were used to (**v 15**). Nehemiah himself "also persevered in the work on this wall" (**v 16**)—not just ordering others around but working hard and showing consistency in the midst of adversity. He says, "We acquired no land." He was not out to get rich. *I didn't buy property,* he is saying, *because I wanted to set the people up to buy it themselves.* Finally, Nehemiah's servants, instead of serving him, were sent to work on the wall (**v 16**). In other words, Nehemiah, like Paul, bent over backward and sacrificed even what would normally be his due to serve as an example to the people (see 1 Corinthians 9; 2 Thessalonians 3:8).

Slave of All

This is a model for us as Christians. We need to come out of our culture's philosophy of entitlement. We need to lay down our rights for the benefit of others and for the glory of God.

In Mark 10:42-44, Jesus said to his followers, "You know that those who are considered rulers of the **Gentiles** lord it over them, and their great ones exercise authority over them. But it shall not be so among you. But whoever would be great among you must be your servant, and whoever would be first among you must be slave of all."

The servant leadership in Nehemiah 5 is beautiful because we see Jesus in it. Nobody did servant leadership better than him. In Mark 10:45 he continues, "Even the **Son of Man** came not to be served but to serve, and to give his life as a ransom for many." He became human and denied himself his rights to his own almighty power for a season; he denied himself his right to life by going willingly to the cross. He did so to put us in a redeemed position before God. That's the greatest example in Scripture of anybody denying themselves their rights for the exaltation of others. Ultimately this was not only for the sake of humans but to glorify the living God, revealing his nature as both perfectly just and perfectly loving.

We all need to learn how to shape our lives to be the servants of others. In marriage, for example, there will be times when you have to forgo your rights. I remember one time when my wife, Yvette, was sick and could not be intimate for nine months. I could have argued that I had a right, based on 1 Corinthians 7:3-4, to say, "Your body is not just yours. Come here." But that wouldn't have made for good intimacy, and it wouldn't have been a good expression of my love for her. I had to surrender my rights to intimacy with her for that time, and pray and vent to God, and not use any illegitimate outlets that might have seemed like they would tide me over but would really have messed me up. God helped me to serve my wife instead of exacting my rights.

Surrendering rights is a deep, deep act of faith. It is not easy. But God will meet us in it. We can be real with him: "I'm struggling, struggling, struggling. But I know that doing things not your way doesn't work, God. So I just need your help." If God is going to call us to deny ourselves and surrender our rights for his glory, we need divine assistance to remain faithful to him and to his mission. When we ask him for help, it will come.

The Fear of God

For Nehemiah, surrendering his food allowances and right to taxation isn't a political move to get something from people. His motivation is the fear of God (Nehemiah **5:15**).

The fear of God, or the fear of the Lord, is an expression of reverential submission to the will of God. It is the beginning of wisdom (Proverbs 9:10)—that is, not a mere first step but the whole foundation of what it means to walk in submission to the Lord. It's not the fear that if you do something bad, something bad will happen to you. Fear of

God does not mean being scared of consequences but respecting the lordship of God in your life. When you fear God, you want intimate fellowship and connection with him, and you don't want anything in your life to be a barricade against that.

That's why it's good to be meticulous about repenting of sin and to consider in every situation whether or not what's happening is for God's glory. When you ignore sin, it doesn't make anything better. It makes it worse. What you have to do is to confess sin, deal with it, and repent of it. Ask for God's help. When you do so, you are saying, "I want to stand in all the reality of you in my life. I don't want anything to get in the way of our relationship."

When you feel that way, when you know you have God, it becomes easy to surrender rights. The more intimate your relationship with God, the easier it is to make sacrifices. It doesn't stop the pain of the sacrifice itself, but it does make your willingness painless.

The Bigger Picture

Nehemiah's message to his people when he surrendered his rights was *What God wants to do in your lives and in this city is more important than my personal preferences and desires.* Fearing the Lord meant taking hold of the bigger picture. He was not just prioritizing the people over himself for humanitarian reasons. He also wanted to further his project of rebuilding Jerusalem, in order to bring glory to God.

Nehemiah chose not to tax the people, which meant that he had to pay for food at his own expense. That doesn't sound too bad. But then he explains, "Moreover, there were at my table 150 men" (Nehemiah **5:17**). Can you imagine having a dinner table with 150 people sitting round it? It means he had a banquet hall, and every day he had 150 people at a banquet. And they were not just eating the bare minimum. Every single day for these 150 people the cooks prepared one entire ox, six of the best sheep, and six birds (**v 18**). Every week that's seven cows, 42 sheep, and 42 birds. Not to mention the wine. This was quite some expense. And it was all out of Nehemiah's own pocket.

These 150 people were "Jews and officials." These were Nehemiah's boys: his entourage of people who helped him to run the province. He was single-handedly providing for 150 people, in order to be able to run things effectively and rebuild the city.

Nehemiah saw the bigger picture: the development of God's kingdom. He wanted to make sure that the people of God were set up well. That was why he stood for justice, didn't exact unnecessary taxes, and persevered in the work on the wall.

> It is God's priorities that matter. My life is about the glory of God and the development of others.

We must ask ourselves: would I do the same? Many of us persevere in personal benefit—earning money, getting fit, enjoying vacations, spending time with friends—but we don't persevere in kingdom benefit, which might involve losing money or respect or spending time with hostile or difficult people. But it is God's priorities that matter. We must expand from a kingdom of me to a kingdom of *he*. My life is about the glory of God and the development of others.

Serving the Nations

Besides the 150 men of Nehemiah's entourage, there were also "those who came to us from the nations that were around us" (**v 17**). He had people from other nations at his table.

Nehemiah was facilitating this daily banquet out of his own pocket, not only in order to minister to God's people but also to minister to **the lost**. Why? Because Israel was always supposed to be a missionary entity. The nations were to be blessed through them (Genesis 22:18).

They were supposed to be an example of what it looks like when God looks after a people, and to reflect his glory. People who were not God's people would come close and see the beauty of God in the life of the people of God, based on the way they interacted with him and the way they treated one another. God's people were to serve those of other nations into the kingdom.

This bringing together of many peoples is part of God's vision for the future new creation. We see the same idea clearly at **Pentecost**, when the Holy Spirit came upon the first disciples, enabling them to speak in many languages. As theologian Daniel Hays points out (quoting the Bible teacher and theologian John Stott), this multilingualism has an **eschatological** significance:

> "Stott summarizes the theological truth of Pentecost by writing:
> 'Nothing could have demonstrated more clearly than this the
> multiracial, multinational, multilingual nature of the kingdom of
> Christ.' Furthermore, Stott continues, this event not only con-
> nects back to Genesis 10 – 12 but points forward to the scene
> depicted in Revelation 7:9, where the redeemed will come from
> every nation, tribe, people, and language."
>
> (From Every People and Nation, p 165; quoting
> John Stott, The Message of Acts, p 68)

If that's the vision of the future we're looking forward to, then caring for others—especially those of other nations, tribes, and tongues—is an expression of gospel-centered values. It is a way of giving your life away instead of taking what you want for yourself. We should begin to say, "God, I want to crack open my life and give it away to others. God, I don't just want to think about my benefit, I want to think about yours."

Seeking Favor

Even though Nehemiah knows how to act decisively and exert coura-geous leadership, his dependence, ultimately, is on God. That's what his prayer is about in Nehemiah **5:19**: "Remember for my good, O my God, all that I have done for this people."

Nehemiah's actions were motivated by spirituality. So it follows that his prayer for favor here is not so much a plea for a reward as an emphatic way of claiming that he has acted in good faith and from right motives. It is a statement of confidence that God is just and judges favorably those who sincerely seek to do his will. In other words Nehemiah is saying, *Please recognize me as one who is meticulous in trusting you and serving you in self-sacrificial ways.*

That's my prayer for my life: that I would be able to say that to the Lord. *God, I really want to do things your way. Remember me favorably as you hand out resources and blessing, because I'm going to use whatever you give me to your glory and benefit.*

Ask yourself honestly: Can I be that bold? Can my prayer life be that bold with God? Do I have a track record with the Lord in which he is used to seeing me use the resources that are placed in my hands for something bigger than myself? And if not, what can I do to start developing one?

To look at it another way, whenever we are given favor and blessing, that is a new opportunity to put God first. When people show us favor, it's really God opening up a door. And he's not opening that door for us to please people but for us to please him and expand his kingdom wherever he has sent us. God gives those who serve him favor. I'm not talking about any prosperity doctrine that says every Christian should be rich. But when God does supply more than our personal needs, it's for the benefit of others, for the development of his kingdom, and to his glory.

Our Lord, in his **incarnation**, did even more. He laid aside the privileges of his deity in order to become our servant to become our Savior (Philippians 2:1-11). Most times we work our lives to prove what we are worth so that we can be served, but Jesus worked his whole life to show himself as the ultimate servant for the glory of God and for our good. Even now he exists to give **intercession** on our behalf (Hebrews 7:25). Even while sitting on the throne, he still functions as a servant. What a motivation that is to be servants ourselves.

Questions for reflection

1. What rights do you have?

2. Is there anything you need to give up in order to serve others?

3. What will you pray for yourself as a response to this chapter?

6. FINISHING THE WALL

Focus matters. You can have all the abilities and opportunities in the world, but if you don't have focus, you'll never get anywhere—not in your life and not in your service of God.

I once listened to a commentator talking about focus with regard to the MMA fighter Brock Lesnar. Lesnar is big and tough and intimidating. But the commentator said, "He's not able to focus while being hit in a ring. I know why: it's because nobody's teaching him how to take a hit." Fighters who aren't used to taking punches don't have their bodies conditioned to absorb hits during a fight and still press through to apply their training.

"If I were his trainer," the commentator went on, "I'd back him up against the wall where he had nowhere to go and just swing punch after punch at him. He would be blinking and flinching at first, but then he would get the rhythm of where the punches were coming from. Then he'd stop flinching in his fights—not because he'd have more skill than he had before, but because he'd have learned how to focus."

Many of us need to learn a lesson like that too. Focus is a very important part of our development as believers. Focusing on Jesus is what enables us to be effective kingdom workers and bear fruit for him.

Take Nehemiah. He is in a great situation. He has a great opportunity. But without focus, he will be taken off-task. He needs clarity of purpose to finish the wall.

Fortunately, God wants to teach us to focus. And he often does so through adversity—like a coach swinging punches at an MMA fighter.

In Nehemiah 6, the building of the wall is almost complete. All of the breaches have been filled. There are just a few openings: the gates which don't yet have their doors (**v 1**). They're almost finished. What happens next is that the enemy turns up the heat.

The Value of the Work

Sanballat and Geshem want Nehemiah to leave the work and the city and come out to meet them: "'Come and let us meet together at Hak-kephirim in the plain of Ono'" (**v 2**). At first this seems like a friendly invitation. Maybe they will be able to negotiate an agreement and an end to hostility. But Nehemiah knows what is really going on: "They intended to do me harm." Sanballat and Geshem are no longer try-ing to attack the work as a whole. Instead they are trying to take out Nehemiah. They think that with him gone, the work will stop.

Nehemiah is not going to be taken in! Yet his own safety is not his chief concern. When he sends messengers back to say he won't come, the message is "I am doing a great work and I cannot come down. Why should the work stop while I leave it and come down to you?" (**v 3**). Nehemiah remains focused.

The only way to be focused is to know and value what God has called us to do. We have to develop an affection for the will of God that allows us to not only know what he wants but also to value it when he shows it to us.

When I was called to **vocational ministry**, I began to understand what Paul says: "Woe to me if I do not preach the gospel!" (1 Corin-thians 9:16). When I tried to walk away from preaching the gospel, I felt this arrest from the Holy Spirit. But when I moved toward it, even though I didn't like that I was going in that direction, peace flooded my soul. That was how I knew, and how I came to value, the will of God for me.

It is interesting that Nehemiah says, "I cannot come down." Geographically, Ono is lower than Jerusalem. But when Nehemiah says, "I cannot come down," I don't think the significance is only geographical. It's a helpful reminder that because when you're focused on anything that's not God's will, even though it may be appealing and attractive in lots of other ways, it is always a step down.

Let's say you're attracted to someone. There's "chemistry." But is that relationship a come-up or come-down? Will he or she lead you toward Christ or away from him? Or let's say you have an opportunity to get more money. A promotion maybe. Ask yourself: what does God get out of your exaltation? If the answer is nothing, then it's not exaltation. It's humiliation.

> Ask yourself: what does God get out of this?

We need to begin to say, "I'm not going to come down in this area of my life. I know that thing over there looks good, but I also know what God has called me to do and what he has focused me on. I know what his word says, and I don't want to do anything outside his word because that's nothing but a come-down."

We cannot ignore the fact that we are engaged in spiritual warfare. We need to know what the nature of the attack is and what practical steps we need to implement to remain focused. In Nehemiah's case, Sanballat, Tobiah, and Geshem the Arab are the visible attackers, but Satan is behind the scenes. Whenever we are hard at work for the kingdom, the enemy will rear his head to attack. We don't wrestle against flesh and blood!

Jesus, however, has the power to deal with such enemies on our behalf. In Matthew 12:29 he tells a **parable** about the devil: "How can someone enter a strong man's house and plunder his goods, unless he first binds the strong man?" The implication is that Jesus himself is the one who "ties up" the devil. Theologian Clinton E. Arnold writes:

> "This tying up ... is best explained by what Christ accomplished on the cross. It was there that Christ shed his blood and made

satisfaction for the sins of the world. Satan thereby lost his ability to justly accuse people because God could extend forgiveness and bring them into a relationship with himself. Paul speaks of this defeat of the powers of darkness in eloquent terms in Colossians 2:15: 'And having disarmed the powers and authorities, he made a public spectacle of them, triumphing over them by the cross [NIV].' Satan has thus been bound, not absolutely, but with respect to those who have entered into a relationship with Jesus Christ. Satan no longer holds these children of God in bondage; they have the power to resist him and undertake the work of the mission."

(*Three Crucial Questions about Spiritual Warfare,* Kindle loc. 840)

Character Assassination

Sanballat sends his invitation four times, and Nehemiah answers him the same way four times. Then "Sanballat for the fifth time sent his servant to me with an open letter in his hand" (Nehemiah **6:5**). Usually a messenger would guard his message with his life because it was only for one specific recipient. The sender would fold or roll the letter and seal it; they'd heat wax, drop the wax on the fold, press a signet into it, and let it dry. This kept the letter secure; it would be obvious if someone had broken the seal. But this letter is unsealed. As he travels from Samaria to Jerusalem, the messenger can share the letter with everybody. Sanballat wants as many people as possible to read his slander against Nehemiah.

"It is reported … that you and the Jews intend to rebel; that is why you are building the wall. And according to these reports you wish to become their king. And you have also set up prophets to proclaim concerning you in Jerusalem, 'There is a king in Judah.'" (**v 6-7**)

When somebody wanted to be a king, they would tell false prophets to prophesy good things about them so that people would exalt them.

So this accusation adds detail to the main slander: rebellion against King Artaxerxes.

I like the way Nehemiah responds. He says, "No such things as you say have been done, for you are inventing them out of your own mind" (**v 8**). He is completely straightforward: *You're lying!*

He adds, "They all wanted to frighten us, thinking, 'Their hands will drop from the work'" (**v 9**). Once again, it's clear where Nehemiah's priorities lie—and what his enemies are trying to do. None of this is really about Nehemiah. It is about God's kingdom being built. Nehemiah knows that the battle is not his but the Lord's. So he doesn't waste words or energy getting upset or defending himself at length.

One of the most difficult things to do in life is to ignore liars and people who slander or undermine us. Over my years in ministry, every time God was about to do a major kingdom work or there were opportunities appearing, there were also people who were used by the enemy to distract us—whether by going to social media and unbiblically venting or by telling other church members blatant lies about the church leadership. There are occasions when responding is appropriate. However, there are also times when our response can add fire to foolishness. If you become too concerned about how people perceive you and you endlessly try to respond to them, you'll drive yourself mad. Martin Luther King said it best:

"Seldom, if ever, do I pause to answer criticism of my work and ideas. If I sought to answer all of the criticisms that cross my desk, my secretaries would be engaged in little else in the course of the day, and I would have no time for constructive work." (from *Letter from Birmingham Jail*)

We can't rebuild and be a part of God's kingdom-building process if we're going to walk in unbridled insecurity. We can be secure in him and make him our focus.

A Little Talk with Jesus

Nehemiah walks by faith in deepening his commitment to the work through prayer: "But now, O God, strengthen my hands" (Nehemiah **6:9**). Of course, it isn't really his hands that he is praying for directly but the state of his heart in the midst of opposition. He needs to be motivated to keep his hands on mission. No heart, no hands!

We have already seen this commitment in chapter 4, as Thomas B. White reminds us:

> "Nehemiah gives us another blueprint. God raised him up as a 'project manager' to recruit a crew to repair the broken walls and burned gates of Jerusalem ... In the face of enemy taunts, and a project that seemed daunting, Nehemiah just kept seeking God's help in prayer and sending his laborers to the wall, one hand working, the other holding a weapon."
>
> (*The Believer's Guide to Spiritual Warfare*, Kindle loc. 1851-8)

Nehemiah has acted with certainty and clarity. He is not afraid. But in **6:9** he prays just in case—as if he doesn't quite trust in his own sense of security. He's saying, *I know everything's all right, but I don't want to stand in my own strength, God.*

When difficulty comes at us, we may find it doesn't actually bother us all that much because we are able to rejoice in Christ. But we should pray anyway—just in case. Sometimes there may be something deeper or more difficult behind what's currently happening, which we don't know about yet and which will be much harder to deal with.

My grandmama used to say, "Just a little talk with Jesus will make everything all right." And she was right. A little whisper to the King of kings and the Lord of lords will break the power of attacks on his mission. You don't have to make a long speech; just shoot up a little prayer. Nehemiah simply says, "Strengthen my hands." We can say to God, "I'm not weary right now, but strengthen my hands." It's like saying, "I want to remain focused. I don't want anything to get in the way of what you have called me to do." That's a prayer we can pray every day.

Subtle Distraction

Nehemiah needs that strength he has just prayed for. Next, it's one of his own people who tries to take him off-focus.

Shemaiah, one of the prophets (that is, someone who hears, or claims to hear, directly from God), says to him, "Let us meet together in the house of God" (**v 10**). He tells Nehemiah, "They are coming to kill you. They are coming to kill you by night." *Come into the temple and bar the doors, Nehemiah. You'll be safe in there.* But Nehemiah says, "I understood and saw that God had not sent him" (**v 12**).

How does he know this? Because he knows his Bible. He knows that it is a sin for him to go into the temple. Nehemiah is not a priest. He is allowed to enter the temple courts, but not the temple building itself. Only priests and temple attendants can go in there. So he answers, "What man such as I could go into the temple and live? I will not go in" (**v 11**).

Shemaiah's plan looks like a prophecy: like hyper-spiritual information directly from God. But it isn't biblically rooted—it contradicts God's law—so Nehemiah knows that it is designed to take him off-focus.

It's obvious how this applies to us. If we don't know our Bible, we will be in danger of being taken off-focus. Read the book and get it into your system! "How can a young man keep his way pure?" asks the psalmist. "By guarding it according to your word" (Psalm 119:9). "I have stored up your word in my heart, that I might not sin against you" (v 11). The Bible keeps us focused. Reading it refocuses us when we are tempted to sin. When we hear advice from people—including those who use Christian lingo to back up what they say, or who sound hyper-spiritual—our first question should be: what does the Bible say?

In the following verses we find out where Shemaiah's "prophecy" actually comes from: Tobiah and Sanballat (Nehemiah **6:12-13**). Their plan is to pay this man to scare Nehemiah and persuade him to fall into sin by entering the temple. This will give him a bad name among the people of God and undermine his leadership.

Shemaiah's attempt to lead Nehemiah into sin is not the only one. **Verse 14** talks about "the prophetess Noadiah and the rest of the prophets who wanted to make me afraid." Yet Nehemiah consistently avoids falling into their traps. He knows what the plan of the Lord is, and he trusts it.

There's yet another example of Nehemiah's unflinching focus on God in **verse 14**. Once again, he chooses not to retaliate or to try to deal with his enemies in his own strength. Once again, he offers up a prayer instead: "Remember Tobiah and Sanballat, O my God, according to these things that they did."

It's tempting to fight for ourselves—to give our opponents a piece of our mind. But the Lord can fight better than any one of us. Nehemiah knows that, and he lets God fight.

Our struggles are more than just our struggles. They are about God, who wants us to reflect who he is. So whatever is happening to you right now—whether it seems good or bad, pleasant or painful—don't let it take you off-focus.

Questions for reflection

1. What do you think is your biggest potential distraction from God's work?

2. When we hear advice from others, how can we discern what comes from God and what doesn't?

3. What steps can you take to keep yourself on-focus for God?

PART TWO

God's Will Is to Finish

"So the wall was finished" (Nehemiah **6:15**).

Finishing things brings glory to God. Have you ever started something that God called you to do, but never finished it? Maybe you are afraid to re-engage with it. Maybe you just ran out of energy. But God wants us to be finishers. We shouldn't just start a bunch of projects. We should finish them—not merely for our own sake or for the sake of the project itself, but because it honors and glorifies him.

But it's not just that the wall is finished. It is finished in 52 days! That's bananas. They finish rebuilding the walls of an entire city in less than two months. What we see here is God meeting the people within their task, enabling them to complete the work, massive though the rebuilding project is. Because they have finished it so quickly, it is noticeable that God is with them. Even those who oppose them have to admit this: they "perceived that this work had been accomplished with the help of God" (**v 16**).

Exposing Hearts

Here's what happens when people hear the news: "All the nations around us were afraid and fell greatly in their own esteem" (**v 16**).

The nations are not afraid because Nehemiah has threatened them or attacked them. They are afraid because of what God has done. They are realizing that God, whose work they are opposing, is sovereign. He is in control of everything, seen and unseen.

The word "esteem" literally means "eye." More than the eye itself is implied: in Hebrew thought, the eyes were the mirror of a person's inner being. The phrase "in your eyes" was equivalent to personal opinion or judgment—the whole way you see things or, in this case, the way you see yourself. The nations seem to have been getting much of their self-worth from the downfall of the people of God. In other words, as they tear people down, they feel better about themselves.

But God exposes where their hearts are, and they fall in their own esteem.

This gives us a lesson too. We had better be careful of the way we see ourselves and the things we value. We need to make sure that our faith and our commitment and our passion are in Christ, and Christ alone. Ask yourself: Am I disappointed when others are raised up above me, or am I happy to see Christ being glorified through others even if that is costly to me? What brings me most joy—is it Christ being exalted, or is it me being exalted?

Opposition Doesn't End

The reason Nehemiah's enemies are so upset about the completion of the wall is that it gives the people in Jerusalem protection. They aren't so vulnerable anymore. That means that they are freed up to develop things within the city itself.

The rebuilding of what is inside the walls means bringing honor to God because a well-built Jerusalem is a better reflection of him. When God's city was in ruins, his people had a bad reputation among the nations around them. But now he is strengthening them, taking away their embarrassment, and giving them the ability to rebuild their dignity.

Many of us need our dignity rebuilt. And God, through his grace, restores dignity to the lives of those who have none. Not only that, but he gives us the ability to enjoy him and enjoy his people and his blessings. He fills us with his Holy Spirit, and he enables us to reflect his glory. As 2 Corinthians 3:18 says, "We all, with unveiled face, beholding the glory of the Lord, are being transformed into the same image from one degree of glory to another. For this comes from the Lord who is the Spirit. " As glory reflecters, through every tough experience we grow in our ability to glorify God more expansively. We are being rebuilt just as Jerusalem was rebuilt.

But in Jerusalem, the completion of this wall of protection does not put an end to hostility—and again the opposition comes from within. Remember the nobles who were oppressing the poor in chapter 5? Now they're sending letters to Tobiah, the enemy of God, telling him what's happening in Jerusalem (Nehemiah **6:17**). They are doing so because they are "bound by oath to him" (**v 18**).

They're related. Tobiah is a son-in-law in one noble family and a father-in-law in another. These families have bound themselves with promises to Tobiah—not just to do with marriage but to do with supporting him more generally and having his support. In other words, they are seeking personal benefit; they are more concerned about their personal kingdom than God's kingdom.

Besides sending letters, these people come to Nehemiah and tell him about Tobiah's "good deeds" (**v 19**). They try to persuade Nehemiah that he is a good man. But in the midst of this pressure from within his own people, Nehemiah has the tenacity to make godly decisions. He knows what Tobiah is really like—he tells us "Tobiah sent letters to make me afraid." He will not bow to the pressure to embrace this man.

The ongoing hostility that Nehemiah experienced even after the wall that protected the city was completed is instructive for us. As believers, we are like a city protected by a wall. By dying on the cross, Jesus has put a protective barrier around us. But for Nehemiah, completing the wall didn't put an end to controversy, challenges, frustrations, or temptations. It won't for us either. When Jesus said, "It is finished," his work of atonement *was* finished—he had fully appeased the wrath of God. He has made his followers safe forever; he has put his Holy Spirit within us, to develop and change us. These things are certain—as is the final redemption of all things. At the same time, though, the pain isn't over, and it won't be until Jesus comes again. We still face trials, temptations, suffering, setbacks, and opposition. We should respond just as Nehemiah did: by putting our trust in the Lord, who has promised to be with us.

Faithful Friends

In chapter 7 Nehemiah takes an inventory of all God's people.

It starts with the appointment of key roles within the city. He appoints "the gatekeepers, the singers, and the Levites" (Nehemiah **7:1**). Then "I gave my brother Hanani and Hananiah the governor of the castle charge over Jerusalem, for he was a more faithful and God-fearing man than many" (**v 2**).

These men have hung in there with Nehemiah—not as "yes men," faithful to Nehemiah himself, but as men who are primarily faithful to God. They can be trusted to make decisions that reflect the heart of God, not the heart of man.

It's people like that whom we need to have around us. 2 Timothy 2:22 says, "Flee youthful passions and pursue righteousness, faith, love, and peace, along with those who call on the Lord from a pure heart." We should not just seek buddies, but faithful and God-fearing people. After all, if someone looks out for God's interests, they will automatically look out for the interests of others.

In Nehemiah **7:3** we see that although the walls are done, there is still a need to protect the city and all that they have invested in the work. So Nehemiah instructs Hanani and Hananiah to maintain guards at the doors and gates of the city.

Now that the wall is rebuilt, the city can be developed. At the moment it is "wide and large" but with few people and no functioning houses (**v 4**). The city needs to be revamped and filled with the people of God. Then it will be a platform to show off who the Lord is. Nehemiah wants to find out: Who is here? What is in place here functionally for God to be glorified through his people?

In the remainder of the chapter, Nehemiah lists the names of all those who have already returned from exile. This is not a new census but a copying-out of a list of names that has been made before; the same list appears in Ezra 2. Nehemiah **7:5** reveals Nehemiah's plan: once he has been through this genealogy, he will gather the people together and enroll them again. We'll come to that assembly in Nehemiah 8.

Before he starts assembling the people, Nehemiah says, "My God put it into my heart" to do so (**7:5**). The census is not just a dry official document that Nehemiah thinks he should make. He has been told to do it by God—by "my God." His plans for the state of Judah flow out of a loving relationship with his God.

We have seen that relationship all the way through the book. Nehemiah is consistently open to God; he constantly seeks his will. So he knows when God is talking to him. It's like being on the phone with someone and forgetting to hang up; the line of communication is always open. Nehemiah lives his whole life in recognition that God is there with him.

Community Formation

As he tries to find out who's who in the people of God, Nehemiah copies out what is written in "the book of genealogy" (**v 5**): "These were the people of the province who came out of the captivity of those exiles whom Nebuchadnezzar the king of Babylon had carried into exile" (**v 6**).

The men of the people of Israel are numbered (**v 7-38**). Then the priests (**v 39-42**), the **Levites** (**v 43**), the singers and gatekeepers (**v 44-45**), and the temple servants (**v 46-56**).

It is striking that the temple worship is at the heart of everything God's people are doing. The farmers and the goldsmiths and the scribes and the builders and all the other people are not listed by role, but the priests, the Levites, the singers, and the temple servants are. That is because these were the ones who were supposed to lead the people in worship. They were there to make sure that there was proper biblical instruction and guidance and to make sacrifices on behalf of the people. They led the people in confession and repentance of their sins and in worshiping the Lord. The life of the community was centered around God, through the work of these leaders.

The people support the work of community formation by accepting financial responsibility for it. **Verse 70** says, "Some of the heads of fathers' houses gave to the work." The heads of the households go through the families under their tutelage, collect resources that are representative of the resources each family has, and give to the work of God.

It's a good principle to follow. Giving shows gratitude for who the Lord is and what he does. We pray, ask the Lord to give us guidance, and regularly honor the Lord with the first of our wealth.

These heads of households give to "the treasury" (**v 71**): that's the temple treasury. The only way the priests were able to be in full-time ministry and to dedicate themselves fully to the tabernacle was because others paid gifts into the treasury.

Who's on the Team?

The last group of people recorded are "the sons of Solomon's servants" (**v 57-59**). These are descended from non-Israelites who served under **Solomon's** rule, whom he enslaved (unlawfully: he was allowed to hire workers but not enslave people) to help build the temple and the city (1 Kings 9:15-23). The descendants of these slaves are now included within the people of God.

Verses 61-65 tell us about another group of people whose identity as part of the people of God is questionable. "Those who came up from Tel-melah … could not prove their fathers' houses nor their descent, whether they belonged to Israel" (**v 61**). There are also some among the priests whose name cannot be found in the genealogies, so they are "excluded from the priesthood as unclean" (**v 63-64**).

Verse 65 may seem strange. What's going on is that since these men don't have the documentation to prove their place among the priests, there has to be some process to bring clarity. Nehemiah restricts them from eating the most holy things—food that priests ate as their portion after the sacrificial rites—as the law instructs (Leviticus 2:3; 7:21-36)—until "a priest with Urim and Thummim should arise."

The Urim and Thummim would be used to inquire of God as to the credentials of those who claimed priestly ancestry. The exact nature of the Urim and Thummim is one of the great mysteries of the Old Testament. What is known is that they were placed in the breast-piece of the high priest and that they were used to discern God's will (see Exodus 28:30; Leviticus 8:8). It has been suggested that they were two small objects, used much like the casting of lots (see Israel Loken, *Ezra & Nehemiah*, on these verses). Nehemiah and the rest of the returned exiles apparently do not have the Urim and Thummim, so they cannot be certain whether these men really should be among the priests. Until it can be proved that they should be, they are excluded from the priesthood.

Although the individuals named here cannot prove their ancestry, they have still been allowed to return with the rest of the exiles. It is probable that they lost proof of their heritage during the chaos that surely existed during the Babylonian invasion and subsequent exile. They are probably now given the same rights as **circumcised** foreigners.

> Who's a member and who's just an attender? Who is ready to represent God's reign?

What we're seeing here is community formation. Who is the covenant community? Who is a member here and who's just an attender in Israel? Nehemiah wants to know who is actually ready to represent God's reign. Not only that, but who is qualified to serve the people spiritually.

We need this in our churches today: a deep level of community formation and commitment. We need to become functioning, unified, devil-destroying communities, impacting the world and transforming the community around us. That only happens when we are identifiable; when we have stood up to be counted; when we are committed to God and to his work. That's what God is calling us to through Nehemiah.

The final verse of this chapter tells us that all these people were scattered across small communities all over the region of Judah. Throughout the land of Israel, there were outposts of God's people. There were worshiping communities—churches, if you will—throughout the region.

The people of God are now able to be more stable. Nehemiah is now referred to as the governor (Nehemiah **7:65**). What a picture of responsible political leadership we are seeing here! Everyone is now going to their ancestral land or has been placed in their assigned locale. Since Levites have no inheritance in Israel because the Lord is their inheritance (Deuteronomy 10:9), they settle in the regions where they are to serve the people (Nehemiah **7:73**). Whether they serve in the temple or in other towns, they all fall into their proper assignments.

As Nehemiah is setting up the infrastructure, he must make sure that the people remember the word of God. We will see more of this in the next section.

Questions for reflection

1. What does it look like to be passionate about seeing Christ exalted?

2. How could it help you to see yourself as like a city protected by a wall (see page 101)?

3. How does this chapter challenge your view of your church and your own place in it? How can you contribute to a culture of commitment in your church?

7. REBUILT THROUGH THE WORD

The people of Israel have finished working on the wall, and now God wants to more effectively work on *them*. All the people of God get together in a worship gathering of sorts, to listen to the Scriptures.

Nehemiah 8 shows us the power of God's word, as the people hear it read and respond to it with worship and weeping (Nehemiah **8:1-12**). As they examine the word, they find out about God's faithfulness—and about the way God has made for them to keep on reminding themselves of that faithfulness. That's the **Feast of Booths**, which they celebrate in the second half of the chapter.

I'm blown away by this passage. Even though we have more access to the Bible in Western contexts than you can ever imagine—translations, transmissions, seminaries, churches, preachers—I believe that there's still a biblical famine. There is a sense in which people trust everything else except the Scriptures. For example, people will sometimes say that the Bible is the final authority. I don't like that terminology: it implies that you try everything else first, and then, when nothing else works, you try the Bible. That's like me going to change the timing belt on my car. I can't do it on my own. What's the mechanic going to say when I take it to him? "If you had come to me a long time ago…" But because I've decided to come to him finally instead of first, now I'm going to owe him a lot more money.

Some of us are like that with God's word. We go to it finally instead of first. Many of us will try to work on our lives ourselves, and we keep messing it up. *I'm gonna get myself together. I'm going to get it done.* It doesn't work! You have to come to the Scriptures. You can't make yourself whole. Wholeness only comes through Jesus and through his word. The Scriptures are what God uses for "teaching, for reproof, for correction, and for training in righteousness" (2 Timothy 3:16).

In Nehemiah 8, that's what the people of God recognize.

Ezra the Scribe

You can't appreciate what's going to happen in this passage until you know who Ezra is and what his heart was for. We see this backdrop in Ezra 7.

"This Ezra went up from Babylonia. He was a scribe skilled in the Law of Moses that the LORD, the God of Israel, had given, and the king granted him all that he asked, for the hand of the LORD his God was on him." (Ezra 7:6)

Like Nehemiah, Ezra had been living in Babylon and was sent by King Artaxerxes to Jerusalem. He was a priest and teacher—as we see in Ezra 7:10:

"For Ezra had set his heart to study the Law of the LORD, and to do it and to teach his statutes and rules in Israel."

Note the order of that. Ezra set his heart first, before anything else. Ezra made his heart receptive to the word of God. Then he studied. Then he also set his heart "to do it." When you have your heart set on the word of God, it becomes a part of the matrix of your life. It changes your value system, your affections, your desires, your direction, your life. Knowing God's word is about letting the word penetrate your own heart first and foremost. That's what was going on with Ezra.

Some people like to talk and preach, but they are not willing to have the grittiness of the glory of God working in their heart through the word of God. Ezra was not one of those people. He set his heart first to study and to do the word of God, and then, finally, he taught Israel.

God's Word Is Revered

Back in Nehemiah 8, all the people of God get together in the square (**v 1**). They go to city-center Jerusalem, down by the Water Gate, and they ask Ezra to get the **Torah**. "So Ezra the priest brought the Law before the assembly, both men and women and all who could understand what they heard … And he read from it facing the square before the Water Gate from early morning until midday" (**v 2-3**).

These people stood on their feet from daybreak to midday, just listening to the word of God being read. Teenagers! Younger kids too! All who had sufficient maturity to comprehend the readings. (In 10:28, there's a similar expression which explicitly says that "all who have knowledge and understanding" included sons and daughters.) Bible scholar John Walton sheds light on how long they stood listening:

"Daybreak" (ha'ôr) is literally "the light" (cf. Genesis 44:3; Judges 16:2; 19:26; Job 3:3–8; 24:14; Psalm 139:11–12; Isaiah 58:8). The KJV translates the word "morning." At 4:21 the KJV translates as "morning" šahar, which actually is the dawn—the light that appears a good hour before sunrise (Psalm 139:9; Proverbs 4:18; Joel 2:2). The people evidently stood for about five hours attentively listening to the exposition of the Scriptures." (*Zondervan Illustrated Bible Backgrounds Commentary: Old Testament*, volume 3, p 439)

Five hours! Nobody preached or taught at this point. Ezra just read. And nobody complained or told him to hurry up. The text does not tell us that people got tired. They were attentive to the word of God (Nehemiah **8:3**). That gives me chills! You have to really hunger for God to stand for his word that long.

That's not the only thing that shows us the people's reverence for the Scriptures. **Verse 4**: "And Ezra the scribe stood on a wooden platform that they had made for the purpose." In other words, before he even went to get the scrolls of the Torah, they built a pulpit. Ezra was above the people when he stood up (**v 5**). They wanted him to be higher than the people as the word of God was being read.

Not just for volume or so that he could be seen—though it was for those reasons—but to help them to have a certain disposition of heart. They were to view the word of God as exalted.

Many older church buildings have a suspended pulpit: a small enclosed platform large enough for one person at a time, placed high with a spiral stair leading up to it. I saw one in a church building I visited in Boston some years ago and heard an explanation of its history. They wanted the pulpit to be the highest place in the church; they wanted the preacher to remember that he was walking to a special place to do something special. The idea was that the word of God would be held in high regard in their midst.

I admire that. Of course, we don't all need to build special pulpits in our church buildings. But we do need to remember to put the word of God in its proper place—to treat it with the reverence it deserves.

God's Word Sparks Worship

In **verses 5-6** Nehemiah tells us a second time about this first reading of the word.

"And Ezra opened the book in the sight of all the people, for he was above all the people, and as he opened it all the people stood. And Ezra blessed the LORD."

Ezra goes to worship his God. Not just any God—"the great God" (**v 6**). Then this worship pours out onto the people. There is spontaneous standing as soon as the Bible is opened (**v 5**). Some people bow their heads, and some people lift up their hands (**v 6**). Some people even lay their faces to the ground. They want to reverence and worship the living God for allowing the word of God to be preserved and kept so that it could penetrate their hearts.

There is no band there, no bass player, no sound system. They are standing in the middle of a broken city. But the word of God has returned. Although the wall is complete, there is still much to be done. They want to rebuild, but they also want to be rebuilt through the word of God. And the word of the great God sparks worship.

Giving the Sense

Next, God's word is read again—but there is a difference this time.

The people have had an intellectual interaction with the word—hearing and studying it. They have had an emotional and passionate interaction with the word—worshiping God. Now they are going to have a volitional interaction with the word. That is, they are going to let it penetrate their lives.

The Levites "helped the people to understand the Law, while the people remained in their places" (**v 7**). They have already read it. But they read it again. These leaders disperse all through the congregation and explain some of the words so that the people can understand the reading (**v 8**). They hold their small-group meetings right there in their church service.

These leaders have a specialized knowledge that effectively helps people to implement what God says. They begin breaking it up and giving the sense clearly. The point is that when the people understand the word, then they can live it out.

I bought a chocolate cake once which literally took me two weeks to eat. It was huge. Pudding on one level, fudge on another level, all surrounded with chocolate mousse, and then covered in whipped cream. It was massively rich. I had to eat it in stages because it was too much for me. And it was delicious. Colossians 3:16 says, "Let the word of Christ dwell in you richly." In other words, the word of God is rich like that cake. It's so rich that you can't just gobble it down. You have to eat that word in stages.

> The word of God is rich: so rich you can't just gobble it down.

In fact, every individual word of God is like a chocolate cake. It should be rich. It's supposed to release spiritual endorphins into our soul. It's supposed to give us what we need to live—and to live for Christ. That is why it is so important to spend time over it and explain it. We need to take it slowly, chew on it, understand it, and let it dwell in us.

Deep Satisfaction

When the leaders start excavating the text and explaining what the word of God means, the people's tears of joy turn into tears of conviction. "All the people wept as they heard the words of the Law" (**v 9**). They recognize that there is a distance between the way they are living and their commitment to the word of God.

But the leaders say, *No!* "This day is holy to the LORD your God. Do not mourn and weep."

Why? Because God wants us to be **convicted** of our sin, but he doesn't want us to stay in our sin. The leaders want to celebrate the fact that God is about to remove the people's sin from them. They are in the seventh month, which is the time of year of the Day of Atonement (**v 2**; Leviticus 23:27)—the time when the priest entered the temple and made sacrifices for the sins of the people. The Day of Atonement was a day not just to deal with sin but also to cleanse the temple: to reset and restore the sacred space (see Leviticus 16:16). This may have been to show that God was giving Israel as a whole nation a new beginning. So it's appropriate that the people are all together here. The nation is being cleansed.

The people are in a state of repentance. If you're repenting without sensing forgiveness, you're going to go into a state of despair. But when you know you have forgiveness, you can worship and have satisfaction in the living King. This is what Nehemiah, Ezra and the other leaders want the people to do. "Go your way. Eat the fat and drink sweet wine and send portions to anyone who has nothing ready, for this day is holy to our Lord. And do not be grieved, for the joy of the LORD is your strength" (Nehemiah **8:10**). In other words: *Don't let your tears be your strength. Don't let your grief be your strength. The joy of the Lord*—which means being satisfied in the Lord—*is your strength.*

The word "strength" here can also mean a mountain or a stronghold. Imagine a mountainous cave in which you can hide from your enemies. When the Bible says, "The joy of the LORD is your strength," it means that you're hiding in something that's bigger than you. You are satisfied with the one who can cover you and take care of you. You're satisfied with the one who has forgiven your sin.

I have heard so many people say words like these: "I searched far and wide, and I looked everywhere for satisfaction, but everything failed me. But when Jesus came and got me and I was able to put my faith in him, my lack of satisfaction stopped. He removed the evil of my soul, and now I'm learning the secret of what it means to be content with the living God."

The more we get to know the great God, the more we are satisfied. That's why the word of God sparks satisfaction with God.

My wife likes to go in this shop called Bath and Body Works. One day I was there with her, and she handed me this stuff in this tube— a shea-butter body cream. I was suspicious. "You want to have me smelling like apples and stuff?" But she grabbed my hands and just squeezed it on. "Ok, rub your hands together." She had to instruct me. I smelled it. It was neutral. So I rubbed it into my hands.

My hands are dry and cracked. But that shea butter went through the cracks and crevices on my hands and began to heal places that I didn't even know needed healing.

When the word of God hits you, it's like shea butter for your spirit. It'll get into the cracks, it'll get into the crevices, and it'll heal wounds you didn't know you had. When you're desperate for God's word, it goes into the deepest places.

That's what the people are finding here in Nehemiah 8. They mourn and weep as they hear the word of the Lord, because they suddenly realize how much they need healing. But even as they start to cry out to God for help, they find that he has helped them. The joy of the Lord is their strength.

I love the fact that worship follows teaching!

Questions for reflection

1. How does this passage challenge your view of the Bible?

2. Is there anything you would like to change about your approach to God's word?

3. How could you grow in the practice of worshiping God after you read his word?

PART TWO

There is strength in remembering God's faithfulness. There is enjoyment and satisfaction. God is willing to enduringly love through all circumstances! His faithfulness is from everlasting to everlasting. But for many of us, the wonder of that hasn't hit us yet.

In Nehemiah **8:13-18**, the people go to great lengths to remember the faithfulness of God.

On the second day, the leaders say to each other, *That's not going to catch us off guard again.* They gather for a little seminary class just by themselves. "The heads of fathers' houses of all the people, with the priests and the Levites, came together to Ezra the scribe in order to study the words of the law" (**v 13**). This is a gathering with purpose. And they discover how distant their existence has been from the living God.

The Feast of Booths

"They found it written in the Law that the LORD had commanded by Moses that the people of Israel should dwell in booths during the feast of the seventh month" (**v 14**).

Leviticus 23 contains the instructions about this Feast of Booths or Tabernacles. This was the last festival of the year, and many called it the Great Feast. The idea was to point back to the days when Israel experienced God's faithfulness in the **wilderness**. It was a reminder of all the sin and grumbling that God had put up with over that time, and how gracious God had been to them even so. It was a celebration of that reality.

There were various aspects of this festival, but the key one for our purposes is in Leviticus 23:42-43: "You shall dwell in booths for seven days. All native Israelites shall dwell in booths, that your generations may know that I made the people of Israel dwell in booths when I brought them out of the land of Egypt: I am the LORD your God."

This festival points first to Israel's birth as a nation. God reminds them that he saved them from Egypt and brought them into a relationship with himself. It also reminds them of the fact that God has been with them in the midst of hardship, and that he provided—and will provide in the future too. In the wilderness, when the people were hungry, God sent them manna. When they wanted meat, God sent quail. When they were thirsty, he brought water out of a rock. God wants to make sure that they remember this track record. When they get around to vineyards and to fruitfulness, he doesn't want them to forget what it was like when times were hard.

God wants us to remember the days of hardship because, when he makes our lives fruitful, when he begins to bless our lives, he doesn't want us to think that we did it on our own. He wants us to always points back to the one who's the source.

Many of us today are used to the American philosophy of pulling ourselves up by our own bootstraps—the idea that nothing will happen if we don't make it happen. But here's the truth: it all comes from him. Everything in our lives. When God provides for us, we must remember that he's the provider—that he's the source of everything. God wants us not to focus on the actual gifts or resources that he gives but to treat them as finger pointers back to him. The Feast of Booths was there to remind the people of God's provision and of his faithfulness to his people, even when they were unfaithful.

> Don't focus on the gifts themselves. Treat them as finger pointers back to God.

When they have read Leviticus 23, the leaders put out a decree: "Go out to the hills and bring branches of olive, wild olive, myrtle, palm, and other leafy trees to make booths, as it is written" (Nehemiah **8:15**). And they do this, "for from the days of **Jeshua** the son of Nun to that day the people of Israel had not done so" (**v 16-17**).

When God's people first celebrated the Feast of Booths, they were fresh from recognizing what God had delivered them from. But the longer they had a relationship with God, the more they forgot about what he had delivered them from. They became less thankful because they were no longer experiencing the level of intensity that they had had in their earlier journey with God. The more abundance the people of God received from the Lord, the more thankless the celebration became over the years, until finally it was forgotten.

But now the people are fresh out of captivity. They have seen Jerusalem half destroyed and built it up again. They have realized that the Scriptures haven't really been taught and put into practice by them as a nation for centuries. Now they are ready to celebrate God's faithfulness properly again.

The Danger of Entitlement

The Feast of Booths seems strange to us today. You don't see Christians building booths out of olive branches every year to remember the passage of the Israelites through the wilderness. But this passage is a call to us all to remember God's faithfulness, no matter what happens in our lives.

The further away we get from remembering what God delivered us from, the more we develop a sense of entitlement—becoming thankless toward the goodness of God and believing that the good in our lives is deserved. That is a form of self-worship. It's something we are especially in danger of in the West today. Many of us haven't had to go through as much hardship as previous generations. And so we end up having a philosophy of entitlement. Instead, we must try to recognize what it took for us to get the things we have.

Nowhere is this more important than when it comes to the gospel of salvation. We have to know what it took to save us. That's why a hell-less gospel is not the gospel. We have to know that the God of holiness and wrath was after us, so that when we get saved, we know that we weren't entitled to salvation but that it has come to us only because of the goodness and mercy of God. "By grace you have been saved through faith. And this is not your own doing; it is the gift of God, not a result of works, so that no one may boast" (Ephesians 2:8-9).

The other problem with entitlement is that it limits our satisfaction to what God provides. We rejoice in the gift instead of the Giver. When that's our habit, how will we respond when God chooses not to provide? Sometimes God ceases to provide for us specifically because he is trying to remove that sense of entitlement out of our lives.

That's why Paul says, "I have learned in whatever situation I am to be content. I know how to be brought low, and I know how to abound. In any and every circumstance, I have learned the secret of facing plenty and hunger, abundance and need. I can do all things through Christ who strengthens me" (Philippians 4:11-13).

We love to quote that last sentence; it feels motivational. But it's not really a "nothing is impossible," "follow your dreams" kind of verse. What it's really talking about is the ability to go through the bumps and bruises of life and still be satisfied with God. When we don't have a lot and we are frustrated because we want something, that's when we should say to ourselves, "Why am I wanting that? I can do all things through him who strengthens me." When the cupboard is empty, when the bank account is low, when the body is in pain, when the mind is depressed, when people around you don't like you, you can do all things through Christ who strengthens you.

So the question is: Where do you draw your strength from? Where do you draw your soul's resources from? We have to be able to learn this secret: that Christ is the greatest satisfier. We must smash the idol of entitlement and be thankful to our God.

God Pours out Revival

When the people had built their booths and remembered all that God had done for them, "there was very great rejoicing" (Nehemiah **8:17**). In other words, revival happened.

Revivals are "times of refreshing ... from the presence of the Lord" (Acts 3:20). The details of the festival show us how revival happened among the people—and how revival happens for us today.

They keep the feast. "Day by day, from the first day to the last day, he read from the Book of the Law of God. They kept the feast seven days, and on the eighth day there was a solemn assembly, according to the rule" (Nehemiah **8:18**).

On the first seven days of the festival, by the Water Gate, they would pour out an offering of water to God. But on the eighth day of the festival, they wouldn't pour any water out. But this didn't mean that there was dryness. There was an enjoyment of his faithfulness. During the Feast of Booths, they would have vats full of wine and barns full of grain. All of the harvest would have been brought in. That meant that the living God had provided rain. Now they were able to celebrate his provision. On the eighth day, they soaked in God's faithfulness instead of pouring out water.

In John 7, Jesus goes up to the Feast of Booths in Jerusalem. And on the last day—the day when there is no water poured out—he stands up and cries out, "If anyone thirsts, let him come to me and drink. Whoever believes in me, as the Scripture has said, 'Out of his heart will flow rivers of living water" (John 7:37-38).

Jesus is the rock that was struck in the wilderness, out of which enough water gushed to satisfy a multitude in the exodus (1 Corinthians 10:4). Jesus was struck for us on the cross, and blood and water came out. Jesus is the living source of satisfaction—the ultimate provision. The Feast of Booths was a good thing, but we can stop celebrating it because the thing that it was pointing to has now come. Jesus Christ is the greatest record of God's faithfulness.

Living water means water that is always fresh. That's what God is for us. He says in Jeremiah 2:13, "My people ... have forsaken me, the fountain of living waters, and hewed out cisterns for themselves, broken cisterns that can hold no water."

The greatest trick of the enemy is to lure us into seeking satisfaction in something else—into building cisterns to hold our own water instead of continuing to go to Christ for his fresh water. The devil wants us to seek satisfaction in sexual activity. He wants us to seek satisfaction in drugs or drunkenness. He wants us to seek satisfaction in wealth or our careers or simply our own pride.

But the living God sent Jesus Christ to be the ultimate satisfier. Jesus said, "Blessed are those who hunger and thirst for righteousness, for they shall be satisfied" (Matthew 5:6). And as we get used to God satisfying our hunger and thirst, we'll have a record of his faithfulness in our lives.

Questions for reflection

1. Where have you seen God's faithfulness in your own life in the past?

2. When you feel discouraged, what can you do to actively remind yourself that God is faithful?

3. Are there any ways in which you have fallen into the trap of feeling entitled? How can you smash this idol in your life?

NEHEMIAH 9 VERSES 1 TO 38

8. FAITHFUL AND UNFAITHFUL

After the celebration of Nehemiah 8, the people assemble again—but this time they are grieving.

Chapter 9 contains an overview of the redemptive record of God in the lives of his people. We see some beautiful things about who God is and what he's done—how he's always been intervening and helping his people.

So why do the people grieve? Because before you can appreciate who God is, you have to know who you're not. This is a moment of collective repentance.

In Western culture, we usually think of repentance as something done by an individual. However, in Scripture we see corporate repentance: a whole nation repenting together. Sometimes this is Israel; God's people were called to live according to the covenant they had made with God, and so repentance was necessary when as a nation they had turned aside from that covenant. But we do also see examples where God calls other nations to repent. For example, he sends **Jonah** to the Ninevites. God has a standard which he calls all peoples to meet, not just his covenant people.

National revival and repentance should be something that we call for in our day—in our own nation. Or corporate repentance at a smaller level than the whole nation. This means that the entire community takes responsibility for individual sins, as well as sins which the entire community participated in together—and turns to Christ for forgiveness. After all, as the church we have corporate prayer, praise, and worship; why not corporate repentance? The New Testament letters—most of which are written to a church or group of believers, not to individuals—contain many powerful examples of corporate calls to repentance (James 4:1-10 is one). Those first Christians would have understood what corporate repentance meant, and so would the people we see here in Nehemiah.

Sackcloth and Dirt

"On the twenty-fourth day of this month the people of Israel were assembled with fasting and in sackcloth, and with earth on their heads. And the Israelites separated themselves from all foreigners and stood and confessed their sins and the iniquities of their fathers." (Nehemiah **9:1**)

The people of God are owning their sin. They have a posture of humility, demonstrated in the sackcloth. That is the burlap which potatoes come in when you buy them in bulk. Burlap is itchy! It would make you feel like you had the chicken pox. The people are clothing themselves with discomfort. They also pick up dirt and sprinkle it all over themselves, anointing their heads with it.

This isn't the first time sackcloth has been used to express repentance, as one commentary describes:

"Sackcloth was a typical sign of mourning and repentance in the Bible. It was a coarse cloth, normally of black goat's hair. It was usually worn next to the skin as a band or a kilt tied around the waist. The symbolic significance of the wearing of sackcloth can be found among the Assyrians, Moabites, Phoenicians and Arameans." (Matthews, Chavalas, and Walton, *The IVP Bible Background Commentary: Old Testament*, on this verse)

If the sackcloth is a way of showing that they are not comfortable in their sin, the dirt represents how dirty they see themselves as being. The message is: "I'm a mess and I'm dirty, but I wish I had some help. I'm uncomfortable because I acknowledge that sin exists in my life."

This is what we should do if we find that we have become comfortable in our sin. Not that we need to get out the potato sacks—but God wants us to clothe ourselves in discomfort. If you're comfortable in your sin, then you're desensitized to the one who created you. We have to be able to acknowledge that we have sin in our lives and that it is a mess. Only then will we ask for God's help and cleansing.

Beware of a comfortable Christianity! There are some preachers out there who will tell you that God loves you and has a plan for your life. That's true, but it's not true if that's the only thing they say. A call to Christianity is a call to discomfort. If we never talk or think about sin, we are living a delusion. Every now and then, we need to feel bad about our sin, because we can't enjoy the Lord until we deal with the mess.

When the SWAT team throws the tear gas in, everyone knows it's over. We need to ask God to throw tear gas into our souls. We need to be flushed out of our mess and brought out with our hands up, ready to surrender ourselves to God. Godly sorrow leads to repentance (2 Corinthians 7:10). Let's take our sin seriously.

> We need God to throw tear gas into our souls and flush us out of our mess.

Next Nehemiah says that the Israelites separate themselves from foreigners (Nehemiah **9:2**). This isn't an attempt to show them how good they are. They are gathering in order to confess "their sins and the iniquities of their fathers." In other words, they are saying to the non-Jews, *These are not your sins to be dealt with. These are our sins.* They are pulling themselves away from those who are not part of the covenant community because they need to deal with their own mess.

Wearing their burlap sacks, covered in dirt, and separated from foreigners, the people are now ready to confess.

The word "confession" in Hebrew comes from a root that means "to throw" or "to cast off." You throw your sins toward God in order to get them away from yourself. That's the sense of it.

But confession also means "to declare." The sense is to tell it fully. It means admitting you are wrong and not anybody else.

Here's how many of us apologize:

"I'm sorry you felt bad about that."

"I didn't mean it that way, but I'm sorry that you..."

"I know I was wrong, but you have to understand..."

But when we truly confess, we are holding nothing and no one responsible except ourselves. We are facing ourselves and how raggedy we are. This is not the time to ask for favor. We need to focus on the unfavorability of ourselves first.

Confession doesn't mean settling for saying, "Whatever I've done, God—I don't know what I've done—forgive me." Confession of sin is making the effort to pinpoint exactly what you are sorry that you have done. When we admit what the sin was and face the reality of that sin—when we have said, "God, I don't want to be delusional"—only then can we turn from that sin. We can't come into a relationship with God until we admit that we're a mess.

That's why God's people spend a quarter of the day doing exactly that. **Verse 3**: "They stood up in their place and read from the Book of the Law of the LORD their God for a quarter of the day; for another quarter of it they made confession and worshiped the LORD their God." As the reading went on, the people would have seen the gaps and absences in their lives in comparison to what God had commanded. It would have been overwhelming for them to hear and see how far their lives had strayed from God's law. Suddenly they would have been clear about what they had done.

The LORD Alone

We need to face up to our sin. But there's a danger in the other direction too. Some of us focus only on our sinfulness.

If someone focuses on their sinfulness all the time, it may look like humility, but it's actually pride. It can be a way of trying to show how spiritual they are—in acknowledging that they're fallen, lamenting their sin. It seems like they have a right view of their standing before God, but it's actually a wrong view. When we are in a relationship with God through Christ, we are no longer just sinners; through the Spirit, we have the righteousness of Christ inside of us.

Even leaving the pride question behind for the moment, if we focus on our sin all the time, it's not good for us! We'll be depressed. We will despair. Instead, we'd better focus on who God is in the midst of our sin.

In **verse 4**, the Levites stand up, and throughout the rest of the chapter they speak about the history of God's people. They recount the disobedience and rebellion of their forefathers. But every time they talk about their sin, they also talk about the goodness of God. Every single time. Why? Because perfect love casts out all fear. Again and again, the people were faithless; but God was always faithful. That means there is hope of redemption for Nehemiah's generation, too.

But the Levite speakers begin by focusing on the attributes of God. Sometimes it helps to think not just about what he's done but about who he is. It makes you begin to say, "He's bigger than this situation. He's bigger than my sin." The more we focus on the massiveness of who he is, the more we actually forget about the inadequacy of who we are.

The Levites command the people, "Stand up and bless the LORD your God from everlasting to everlasting" (**v 5**). The people are being told to "bless the LORD", but the truth is that human praise isn't enough to prop God up! He exalts himself. That's why the Levites next say, "Blessed be your glorious name, which is exalted above all blessing and praise." God is exalted already. People just participate in his exaltation.

What is God like? He's eternal—"from everlasting to everlasting." He is not limited and bound by time. That helps in the midst of their confession of sin—because their sin is in time, but God exists outside of time.

He is unique. "You are the LORD, you alone" (**v 6**). This means that God is sovereign—he has a unique level of power. "You have made heaven, the heaven of heavens, with all their host, the earth and all that is on it, the seas and all that is in them; and you preserve all of them; and the host of heaven worships you."

"The heaven of heavens" is a way of talking about the place where God's dwelling presence can be safely unveiled. God is everywhere, but we don't see him, because it would kill us. These earthly bodies can't withstand the glory of God. That's why 1 Timothy 6:16 says he "dwells in unapproachable light." There is a place where his glory is fully revealed.

The "host" of heaven means God's army of angels. These beings, more powerful than us, who can see God, spend their time worshiping God. He is God alone. He is more glorious than we could imagine.

The Covenant-Keeper

But God is not a far-off being. He may dwell in unapproachable light, but that does not mean he doesn't approach us. He is the LORD alone, the sovereign Lord; but he's also "the God who chose **Abram**" (**v 7**). He's the God who comes near.

The Levites now begin to talk about God as a covenant keeper—a faithful God who makes promises to his people and keeps them. They start with the covenant he made with **Abraham**.

In Genesis 15 God made an unconditional covenant with Abraham. He promised to give him as many offspring as the stars. He promised that Abraham would possess the land that he had been called to live in.

To ratify those promises, God told Abraham to offer some sacrificial animals. Abraham cut them in half. Usually, when two people made a covenant (a binding agreement) together, they would cut the sacrificial victim in half and walk between the halves together. But that didn't happen in God's covenant with Abraham. Instead Abraham went to sleep, and he saw fire passing between the halves of the sacrifice. That was the Lord! It was God that walked through the sacrifices—on his own. He was promising to be faithful, no matter what. There were no conditions for Abraham to meet. His sin would not overtake God's faithfulness.

This unconditional covenant was not just a covenant with Abraham alone. It was for his offspring. As the Levites say in Nehemiah **9:8**, "You … made with him the covenant to give to his offspring the land."

So next they speak about Abraham's offspring. They fast-forward to the time of the exodus (**v 9-15**). God rescued his people out of Egypt. He faithfully protected them as they fled through the Red Sea (**v 9-11**). He faithfully guided them through the wilderness (**v 12**): the pillar of the cloud and the pillar of fire went before God's people and let them know when they should be still and when they should move. He also faithfully provided for them. He provided for them spiritually, making a new covenant with them at Mount Sinai and giving them "right rules and true laws, good statutes and commandments" (**v 13**). He provided food and water when they were hungry and thirsty (**v 15**).

God was incredibly kind to Abraham's descendants. But, as we're about to see, they did not do much to deserve it.

Questions for reflection

1. What could corporate repentance look like in our day—in the church, and in a secular community?

2. Do you think you are more in danger of failing to take your sin seriously or of focusing on it too much?

3. How does the way Nehemiah talks about God in this passage help you to get the right view of your sin?

RT TWO

The Sins of the Fathers

In **verse 16** the Levites start to recount the unfaithfulness of their ancestors. They're continuing what started at the beginning of the chapter, where all the people "confessed their sins and the iniquities of their fathers" (**v 2**).

This doesn't mean they are blaming their fathers for their own sin. No: they are acknowledging the ways in which they themselves have continued to walk in the ways of their fathers. And they are lamenting and taking ownership of the sins of the past.

Verse 16 takes us back to the time of the exodus once more. "They and our fathers acted presumptuously and stiffened their neck and did not obey your commandments."

Acting presumptuously means having a sense of entitlement in the midst of your sin. These people were so delusional that they were still demanding blessings from God even though they were in a mess. They thought God owed them something, no matter what they did. That's a victimization philosophy of life: not admitting your sin but blaming it on other people. Thinking you're entitled to blessings because everything you've done wrong was the fault of someone else and not yourself.

Maybe someone has given you a hard time. That person is sinful, and that sin is serious. They need to deal with it. But that doesn't give you a green light to follow in their sin. We are all still responsible for our own actions. If we fall into the trap of thinking of ourselves only as victims and not as responsible in our own right, we will end up walking presumptuously through life, being angry with God. We'll think that our own sinful actions shouldn't be dealt with and that God owes us something. And when we walk around like God owes us something, we're in trouble.

Of course, God had promised to bless the Israelites. He had promised to give them the land. He had promised to make them his own people.

But they started taking these promises for granted. They "were not mindful of the wonders that you performed among them" (**v 17**). They had such a sense of entitlement that they were unable to see even the powerful miracles that God did in their lives! "Oh, that was nothing. Do something else." Their sin had caked their eyes up. They forgot that all God's faithfulness was a gift that they didn't deserve.

And so they stiffened their necks. This phrase can be used of an ox. An untrained ox wants to be out with the cows, not working for humans. So when the ox-drivers try to put the yoke on his neck, he stiffens it. They try to push him, but he's not going anywhere. He doesn't want the person that owns him to move him anywhere. That's what it means to be stiff-necked.

Or it's like one of those pitbulls that are so stubborn that they have to have a chain on them instead of a regular leash. You see owners getting pulled all over the place by these stiff-necked dogs who just want to do what they want to do.

If we're disobedient, we are trying to treat God like that. We're trying to go where we want to go. But God is not like a human owner that gets dragged around. You can't stiffen your neck against the living God. You won't win.

God Bore with Them

The people were unfaithful, but God was faithful. That's the headline in Nehemiah 8. In **verse 17** the Levites add, "But you are a God ready to forgive, gracious and merciful, slow to anger and abounding in steadfast love, and did not forsake them."

The Israelites created the golden calf and presented it as their own God: "Your God who brought you up out of Egypt" (**v 18**). That was a major insult to the glory, majesty and work of the Lord. The legacy of their offenses against the Lord was great.

But so is his propensity to forgive. God kept on guiding his people (**v 20**). He kept on providing for them (**v 20-21**)—spiritually, giving his Holy Spirit to instruct them; and physically, giving food and water and even making sure that their clothes didn't wear out. That is how detailed the faithfulness of God was for the people in the wilderness. They had the same pair of sneakers for 40 years!

The Levites don't stop with the exodus generation. Next they move on to the generations that took possession of the promised land. From the grumbling in the wilderness to the anger of Moses to the sin of Achan, God continued to be faithful: to take his people's sin seriously, yet to go on providing for their needs.

When God made an unconditional covenant with Abraham, he promised land and blessing to his descendants (Genesis 15:5, 13-14). In Nehemiah **9:22-25**, the Levites show how these promises to Abraham were fulfilled. It is clear how committed God is to Abraham and his family. We see him giving kingdoms, establishing boundaries, multiplying descendants, and much more.

However, **verses 26-30** reveal once again the people's disobedience. They rebelled against God and committed great **blasphemies** (**v 26**). This caused curses to come upon them. Since the covenant of the law was a conditional covenant, whenever it was violated, the children of Israel would experience enormous consequences (see Deuteronomy 28). They were handed over to their enemies, experiencing oppression and domination by other nations (Nehemiah **9:27**). Yet, as promised, when they repented and turned back to the Lord, he responded in mercy and provided deliverers (**v 28**)—this is a reference to the **judges** in the book of Judges.

Once the people had experienced relief, did they keep on obeying God? No. Yet again they returned to their folly (**v 29**). And the cycle continued.

God is beyond gracious to us. Even after we commit the most heinous of acts against him, he still finds a way to be loving and compassionate towards us. The Israelites were consistently insolent and rebellious—but what is amazing is that God would never utterly destroy them. Even in their unrepentant state, God had compassion on them and did not give them all that they deserved. Sound familiar?

Who God Is

"You are a gracious and merciful God" (**v 31**). The reason God did not destroy the Israelites is because of who he is. This verse is a shorter version of **verse 17**, which is a statement of who God is that appears again and again through Scripture:

"You are a God ready to forgive, gracious and merciful, slow
  to anger and abounding in steadfast love, and did not forsake
  them."

God did not just provide for his people materially. He was ready to forgive. That means that he was willing to allow the wrongs of the past never to count toward their relationship with him again. Or, to put it simply, he reconciled them to himself. And he's ready to do that at every point in time. This is who he is. He is gracious and merciful—always. Imagine if all your friends, all your family, and everyone in your church sinned against you regularly, badly, and all at the same time. I don't know if I would be able to handle the anger that I would have! But God is slow to anger. All of his people sin against him regularly, yet he puts his anger in neutral.

He does it, of course, through Christ. God had to satisfy his own wrath. He satisfied it through Jesus Christ, whose death fully satisfied all the righteous demands of God against the sinner.

That means that we can confess our sins in the knowledge that we don't have to pay for them. If we are trusting in Christ, God put all of our sin on him. When he crushed Jesus, he crushed our sin. But even though it's paid for, he wants us to come before him to acknowledge our sin. It would be delusional to say we don't have sin—to pretend that everything's all right and to demand a blessing. But the type of relationship we have with God is one where God can look at our mess and still love us, because he has taken care of it through Jesus.

Now, Therefore

Verse 32 highlights God's character yet again. When we are disciplined, we can tend to question God's integrity instead of our own—
How could you let this happen to me?—but the Levites know the truth. As they turn to make their request to God, they begin by acknowledging that his integrity is perfect. He is "the great, the mighty, and the awesome God, who keeps covenant and steadfast love."

Then they ask for God's help. They have already recounted the hardships of the time of the exodus and the judges; now they quickly list all the trials the Israelites have gone through since then (**v 32**).

But they also speak honestly of the discipline of the Lord. "You have been righteous in all that has come upon us ... we have acted wickedly" (**v 33**). In doing so, they acknowledge that God is innocent and right in his judgments and discipline toward them. For generations, there have been sin patterns, and those sins have had consequences that have ravaged them. Yet in those very consequences, the Levites see the loyal love of God and his patience toward them throughout every generation. **Verse 34** says that God gave warnings that were ignored by the leadership and the people. This is how we can understand the punishments God gave the Israelites—as warnings.

> In God's punishments for sin, they see his loyal love and patience.

My parents were strict disciplinarians. But they always gave warnings. They gave me the household law, they warned me to keep it, and when I disobeyed, they gave me a chance to repent. It was persistence in disobedience that led to disciplinary action. That's no different than our God.

By recounting this history, the Levites are saying, *We are finally listening to your warnings. We are finally ready to obey.* They are asking God for help, but they are being honest about their past. You know someone is truly repentant when they don't blame God for the circumstances that they placed themselves in. True repentance sees the consequences of one's sin and lets the Spirit do his work of drawing the heart back to the Lord again.

Not doing things God's way, as we can see, sucks. But returning to the Lord is a possibility for those who have gone astray. Theologian Anthony A. Hoekema said it well:

"Rich promises are attached to such returning to the LORD. When God's people do this, God will hear from heaven, forgive their sin, and heal their land (2 Chronicles 7:14); the LORD will have mercy on them and abundantly pardon (Isaiah 55:11); and the LORD will prevent their death (Ezekiel 33:11)."

(Saved by Grace, Kindle loc. 1740-41)

Knowing this, the Levites are now ready to make their request to God—to ask for his mercy and provision once again.

They state their difficulties clearly. "Behold, we are slaves in this day" (Nehemiah **9:36**). They have no king or real government of their own but are subject to Artaxerxes. They labor in the fields, but its produce goes to him. "They rule over our bodies." That word "bodies" is used only thirteen times in the Old Testament, and it characterizes the human being in weakness, oppression, or trouble (e.g. Genesis 47:18–19). It is also used of a "corpse" (1 Samuel 31:10, 12; Psalm 110:6; Nahum 3:3) or a "carcass" (Judges 14:8–9). The Levites are possibly talking about the fact that the Persian rulers drafted their subjects into military service. In other words, the Jews were just cannon fodder. No wonder that they conclude, "We are in great distress" (Nehemiah **9:37**).

Sealing the Covenant

Verse 38 features some heavy commitment language: "a firm covenant," "a sealed document." Something really important is being done here. They are rededicating themselves. God, by his grace, is re-ratifying their commitment to the covenant.

133

As we saw in the last chapter, this covenant does not inaugurate their relationship with God. They already have a covenant with God through Abraham. But this is a different type of covenant than the one God made with Abraham. That covenant was an unconditional covenant. That means they didn't have to do anything to get into this relationship with God. He did it all. However, the people are now making a conditional covenant.

Make no mistake: the unconditional covenant still exists. God makes a way for his people to have relationship with him which has nothing to do with their merits. There is no potential in any human that makes God want to put his affections on them. God just decides that he's going to put his affections on them.

So the unconditional covenant can't be overridden by the conditional covenant that is now being made. The conditional covenant is made in response to the unconditional commitment that already exists between God and his people.

This reality is the same when it comes to the new covenant, which is the one we are under today. The new covenant, of course, is in Christ's blood. God did not wait till we got it right to send Christ. Before the foundation of the world, he decided that he was going to make a covenant with us whether we liked it or not. Christ lived the life we can never live, died the death we can never die, and was raised up from the grave that we could never ourselves rise from (1 Corinthians 15:21-23). That is an unconditional covenant. All we have to do is accept it.

However, as the saying goes, "Salvation costs you nothing, but discipleship costs you everything." In response to the fact that we're in a relationship with God, we make a conditional covenant with him. We say, "Because I'm in a relationship with you, I'm going to serve you."

So although we're reading in Nehemiah about the old covenant, not the new covenant, there is an essential continuity. To gain a relationship with God, we don't do anything. But there is an additional aspect to the covenant that we make with God that does have conditions, as he calls us to live our lives for him and to walk in his ways.

It's a little like a married couple making vows at their wedding. Imagine that a man and woman have fallen in love. They say, "I love you." They get engaged. They go through premarital counseling. They're released from pre-marital counseling. Then they start working on the wedding. They choose a place, they book the banquet hall and the church, they ask a preacher, they invite their friends and family, they pick out decorations and have dresses and suits made. They're excited. Maybe they write their own vows. They discuss what music the bride is going to come in to. After they've done all this work, they finally make it to the altar and say, "I do." Then they head to the reception. They dance. They eat. They make speeches. Then the newlyweds go to their hotel room.

Imagine that in the morning they say, "Well, that was a great day." And they just walk away from each other.

Wouldn't that be weird?

But isn't it weird that many people profess to trust in Jesus Christ as their Savior and then live their lives just the same as if they hadn't? It's like saying, "All right, I've got fire insurance, I'm good"! But that's not the point! When we are in a covenant with God, his love for us woos us into fulfilling the vows that we have made to him.

Those vows are what we will see in Nehemiah 10.

Questions for reflection

1. When in your own life have you experienced God's faithfulness despite your own unfaithfulness?

2. How does God warn us about our sin today?

3. What would it look like for you to pray in the way the Levites do in this passage?

9. SACRIFICIAL COMMITMENT

Joining Together

After getting exposed to God's word in a significant way in chapter 8 and confessing sin in chapter 9, it is time for the people to walk in a sense of covenant renewal—or, as the old church would say, "rededication." They begin with vows. The people are making a major recommitment to God and getting the land back in order. To say that this is significant is an understatement! In many ways this is Israel being re-established as a covenant nation, even though they are still under Persian occupation.

It is not just the leaders listed in **10:1-27** who sign up to this covenant. "The rest of the people, the priests, the Levites, the gatekeepers, the singers, the temple servants, and all who have separated themselves from the peoples of the lands to the Law of God, their wives, their sons, their daughters, and all who have knowledge and understanding join with their brothers, their nobles" (**v 28-29**). All of them—everybody who can understand what they are doing—make a commitment to keeping the covenant.

They "join with" one another. This is a community. They don't see themselves as having only an individualistic relationship with God. They are God's people, together.

The same applies to us. Each person's individual trust of Jesus Christ as their Savior brings them into a community, the church. That means we can't say, "I love God, but I hate God's people." Nor should we seek to benefit from the church without being part of the community of the church. Being in a covenant with God means giving our lives sacrificially to his people.

Much of our lives is tailored to our own personal preferences. On our phones, we get rid of the apps we don't want, we find new ones we do want, and we move them from page to page, according to our personal needs. But don't fall into the trap of thinking of the community of God as an app store! We should have Christ-centered lives, not choice-centered lives. It should not be up to us to choose whether or not we want somebody to challenge us; whether or not we want to listen to this word; whether or not we will love a particular person.

> Don't think of the community of God as an app store!

Notice who is joining together here in Nehemiah. There are men and women, leaders and servants, old people and young people. And, significantly, these people are joining "with their brothers, their nobles." Remember chapter 5? The nobles were the people who were oppressing the poor. The nobles were the people who didn't want to serve. But now they are "brothers." That's amazing.

Together, all the people "enter into a curse and an oath to walk in God's Law" (**10:29**). In other words, they say something like this. *I swear that I will walk according to God's law. And if I don't, let me be cursed.*

Covenant agreements in the ancient world routinely included blessings for keeping the covenant and curses for breaking it. God's covenant with Israel through Moses was presented in the same terms (see Deuteronomy 27:15-26; 30:19). The people in Nehemiah followed this same pattern, taking it for granted that the breaking of the oath would incur a curse, which would be some punishment or judgment from God.

Now this is something which doesn't translate exactly to the new covenant. We can't go around cursing people! It's different because

Jesus cancels out the curses. "Christ redeemed us from the curse of the law by becoming a curse for us" (Galatians 3:13). So now, when we sin, no curse comes upon us. The curse came upon him on the cross.

However, there is a way in which curses translate and are relevant for us. It's about accountability. Curses held people accountable to the covenant. When you weren't behaving the way you should, a curse would remind you that you were out of step and call you to repentance.

There are no curses anymore, but there are consequences for sin, and we do still need accountability. All of us need some people in our lives to challenge us—to tell us about how much of a mess we are! This is a loving thing to do. Why not make an intentional agreement with a few people you trust and admire, people who are maturing in their faith? Give them permission to rebuke you if you need it. They're not pronouncing a curse on you, but you are still putting yourself in a vulnerable place, just as the people in Nehemiah's time are putting themselves in a vulnerable place when they "enter into a curse and an oath."

That takes sacrifice. But it is vital.

The Commitments

Nehemiah **10:30-39** outlines the commitments the people of God are making for themselves. This is a community pledge that presupposes a detailed knowledge of God's law. Submission to the authority of God's word is the unmistakable principle at work.

This post-exile community was experiencing many problems, both **ethical** and religious. The first step toward solving these problems was a commitment by the whole community to submit to the authority of God's **revelation** as found in the Scriptures. The same is true for God's people today. This commitment to the authority of Scripture must be applied to present situations, for "true religion cannot be merely general principles" (F.C. Holmgren, *Ezra and Nehemiah*, p 138). The principles must be applied to specific actions and decisions.

First, the people make a family commitment. They promise, "We will not give our daughters to the peoples of the land or take their daughters for our sons" (**v 30**).

God has already called the people to this (Exodus 34:11-16). The reason was this: *If you marry unsaved people, it's going to skew your commitment to me.* So they commit themselves and promise that they are not going to give their children in marriage just to anyone. This isn't just about the marriage itself. It is about the spiritual trajectory that they are setting up for their families. They want to make sure that their children know God and love him.

Too many parents today are too passive when it comes to their children. They say, "When they become teenagers, I don't want to get too involved in their lives. That might make them reject me—and God."

Of course a parent shouldn't try to control their child's life. That's God's job. But we should be concerned about the lives of our children. We should be nosy. We should get to know the boys who want to date our daughters and the girls who want to date our sons. We should not give our sons and daughters away to just anyone! We want them to be believers, and we want to give them to believers. We should be passionate about this.

This isn't just a promise being made on behalf of sons and daughters; they are making the covenant too, at least if they are old enough to "have knowledge and understanding" (Nehemiah **10:28**). This reminds us that young people and children must be included in community commitment.

Second, the people make a faith commitment: they agree to honor the Sabbath. **Verse 31**: "If the peoples of the land bring in goods or any grain on the Sabbath day to sell, we will not buy from them on the Sabbath or on a holy day. And we will forego the crops of the seventh year and the exaction of every debt."

They are committing to the weekly Sabbath, when they are supposed to rest from their work. They are also committing to the sabbatical year: the rule that every seven years there would be a whole year of rest for the land (Leviticus 25:3-4). They are committing to the year of Jubilee: the releasing of debts which happened every fiftieth year (Leviticus 25:8-10, 13-33). And they are committing to keep various other holy days.

This is not just committing to a day. They are committing themselves to walking by faith. That is what it takes to agree not to work—because not working, in that culture, meant not earning anything.

Unbelievers would keep working on the Sabbath day and in the sabbatical years. They would grow food and buy and sell and do everything that normally the people of God would have done themselves. But the people are promising not to take part in those things on the Sabbath. They are committed to resting when God commands them to rest.

Once again, this is painfully relevant today. We live in a culture of work. We love to be busy. We like to think that we are getting stuff done. But "unless the LORD builds the house, those who build it labor in vain" (Psalm 127:1). The Lord "will neither slumber nor sleep" (Psalm 121:4). That means that while you're resting, God's working. You don't need to be afraid.

Some of us need to learn how to take a break—in Jesus' name. We need reflective spiritual time where we allow the Lord to refill us. Our lives should include times where we reflect on the goodness of God. So ask yourself: When was the last time the Lord really spoke to me? When did I last pause enough to really listen to him? In order to walk in biblical commitment to God, we are going to have to pause our lives—to say yes to him and say no to some other stuff. We need to stop and remember the Lord.

The Service of God

Third, they make a financial commitment. "We also take on ourselves the obligation to give yearly a third part of a shekel for the service of the house of our God" (Nehemiah **10:32**).

They obligate themselves. They don't leave it up to the Levites and the priests and the temple servants to sort out everything that the temple needs to run. They make themselves personally responsible.

Verses 32-39 are all about this financial commitment to the temple. First, they promise to pay for the showbread (**v 33**). This was twelve loaves of bread, replaced every week. It was also called the bread of the Presence. It represented the beauty of God's presence among the people. They also promise to pay for the regular offerings and feasts "and for all the work of the house of our God." You can read more about the different types of offerings in Leviticus 1 – 5. But the most important type of offering to note is the sin offering, "to make atonement for Israel" (Nehemiah **10:33**).

By God's grace, when a sin offering was given, it removed the wrath of God. That's propitiation. It also removed the guilt of sin. That's expiation. When you have both of these, you have atonement: literally "at-one-ment." You're able to enjoy fellowship with God all over again. So the people are promising to make sure that they can continue to be in relationship with God. They provide the resources for the offerings which deal with their sins and the sins of those who will come into the nation.

But notice it says sin "offerings", plural. These offerings had to be made over and over and over again. That's not true anymore. Jesus "has no need, like those high priests, to offer sacrifices daily, first for his own sins and then for those of the people, since he did this once for all when he offered up himself" (Hebrews 7:27). He is our one-time sin offering.

So what is the equivalent of paying for temple resources for us today? It is resourcing the church to making sure that the sacrifice of Jesus is proclaimed. Our resources must go toward the proclamation of the gospel locally, nationally, and internationally. That is how these verses apply to us. We must give money to the work of the church.

The people will pay for these things by bringing their own produce. "We obligate ourselves to bring the firstfruits of our ground and the firstfruits of all fruit of every tree … the firstborn of our sons and of our cattle … the first of our dough" (Nehemiah **10:35-37**).

Do you see the repetition—firstfruits, firstborn, first? It means they give the best. It means that they don't start off by thinking of what they want or need, and then give the leftovers to the Lord. It means that before they even pay their bills, they give the best to the Lord. God wants us to take the resources that he's given us and use them for kingdom mission; and he wants us to think about that first, before anything else.

They also promise tithes (**10:37-39**). This means ten percent of income. These tithes pay the salaries of the Levites, priests, singers, and other temple servants. Again, this is paid so that the work of the temple can continue.

The last part of **verse 39** says, "We will not neglect the house of our God." This is what it all boils down to—for us as well as them. The house of God is not a building. It's a people. Our desire must be to make sure that the **saints** are **edified**, God is glorified, and lost people are evangelized. That's our goal. We want to make sure that there's nothing missing in our churches. And the gospel demands that we obligate ourselves to take responsibility for this. We must live in the light of the covenant he has made with us. After all, if God can sacrifice his best for us, why can't we sacrifice our best for him?

Questions for reflection

1. What does a choice-centered attitude to church look like? How can you make sure you are Christ-centered instead?

2. How committed are you to family, to rest, and to the service of God? What steps could you take to commit yourself more fully?

3. How might you explain to someone why these commitments are so worthwhile?

PART TWO

After God's people have got through the first wave of what needed to be done, they have to get themselves in order.

Jerusalem is bombed out. It is ruined. Nobody wants to live there. So they have to **cast lots**. They put the names of all their families in a hat and draw out names. If your family is drawn, you have to live in Jerusalem.

"The rest of the people cast lots to bring one out of ten to live in Jerusalem the holy city, while nine out of ten remained in the other towns. And the people blessed all the men who willingly offered to live in Jerusalem" (**11:1-2**).

Remember, Jerusalem was supposed to be the model city, the representation of God. But it wasn't just the structures and the buildings and the temple and all of those things that were representative of God. It was the people. That's why Jesus said, "A city set on a hill cannot be hidden" (Matthew 5:14). He wasn't talking about a building, chairs, or sound equipment. He was talking about people.

In today's context, then, we are calling for and asking people to commit themselves to the church. The people of God are the new Jerusalem. We should be a city within a city—representing God's reign to the people around us. We should obey God's call to live in this new Jerusalem.

In Nehemiah's context, though, where Jerusalem is the literal, physical city, not everyone is going to squeeze in there. Only one tenth of the people settled in the city itself. It's important to note that this tenth didn't just include those who were dedicated to temple service. Some of these lived out in the villages (Nehemiah **11:3**), while some of the other people lived in Jerusalem (for example, some descendants of Judah and Benjamin, **v 4-7**). There was no hierarchy whereby the spiritual elite lived in Jerusalem and everyone else lived in the other towns. The professional religious workers lived and worked among all of the people and not in a vacuum where they were removed from the rest of society.

Nehemiah next lays out all the people who did live in Jerusalem (**v 4-24**). Lists like these function as reminders to us that these were real people—real individuals. So far we have often seen the people function as a whole: a singular character who acts and reacts, initiates and responds. But here we read the people's names. It's a reminder that each person has his or her own place in God's plan.

We see that too in the way Nehemiah orders the list of names. It's clear that everyone has their role. There are the "valiant men" or "men of valor" (**v 6, 8, 14**), who presumably defended the city. There are those who worked in the temple, taking care of "the work of the house" and "the outside work of the house of God" (**v 12, 16**) respectively. There's the man who led the praise (**v 17**) and the men who were in charge of singing (**v 22-23**). Each group has its leaders and overseers. And then there's Pethahiah (**v 24**), who seems to have been some kind of ambassador to the king on behalf of the Jewish people. From the highest rung to the lowest, there's order and organization in the way things are run.

Nehemiah doesn't neglect those who live outside the city, although he doesn't list them by name—it would have taken too long. Instead he lists the different regions with each of their villages (**v 25-36**). They've taken possession of the whole of Judah—all the land that was once ruled over by the kings of Judah, from Beersheba in the south to the valley of Hinnom in the north (**v 30**). At last, the people are where they should be.

> At last, the people are where they should be.

Ordering the Leadership

The next thing Nehemiah puts in order is the ministry leadership. The lists in **12:1-26** represent several generations. Jeshua or Joshua was the high priest who returned with Zerubbabel to rebuild the temple, before Nehemiah's time. **Verses 1-9** list the names of those who were

priests and Levites during Jeshua's tenure. Next, **verses 10-11** intro-
duce us to Jeshua's son, and his son, and his son—all the way down
to Jeshua's great-great-great grandson, Jaddua. Then **verses 12-26**
list the names of the priests and the leaders of the people during the
lifetime of each of these men.

What we're seeing here is that spiritual organization was the
foundation of all other forms of organization. Political, economic,
geographical, and family structures all came under and were to be
influenced by the spiritual. No other era in Israelite history needed
organization more than this second temple period, where effectively a
whole new nation was being set up—but they had to start by getting
their spiritual lives in order. And they had to continue that way. This
is why it was so important that multiple generations of priests were
named. The setting up of the priesthood and its legacy meant that
the people would keep being helped to look Godward. That was how
they would prevent further judgment and experience healthy fellowship with the Lord as a community. At least, that was the hope.

Dedicating the Wall

Verse 27 takes us back to the city wall. It was completed back in Nehemiah 7, but it hasn't yet been dedicated. God first wanted to work
on his people. So they have completed a census; they have settled in
their towns; they have heard the reading of the law and celebrated
the Feast of Booths and confessed their sins; they have made a new
covenant with the Lord. Now they are ready to celebrate what has
happened in their community.

> "At the dedication of the wall of Jerusalem they sought the Lev-
> ites in all their places, to bring them to Jerusalem to celebrate
> the dedication with gladness, with thanksgivings and with sing-
> ing, with cymbals, harps, and lyres."

They are ordering themselves as a community of worshipers. This is
not just a celebration of a mile-marker in their personal lives. God
has moved the community forward as a whole. That is what they are

celebrating. They know how to say, *God, we knew how bad it was and how it looked like this wasn't going to happen, but we got a word from you and knew we were called to do this. The walls were messed up, our lives were messed up, the whole land was messed up, but all of a sudden you've given provision, and we want to stop and say thank you.*

In our own days, as church has become more informal, there is a feeling that not much is sacred and celebrated anymore. Older ways of doing things might have had too many festive days and at times could feel a bit too formal, but they did show an understanding of sacred and God-ordained moments, and they built the recognition of those moments into the rhythm of the church year. I hope that we too can find practical ways to appreciate and celebrate the Lord's work in and through his people. Whether it's a ministry anniversary, a church anniversary, the dedication of new ministry space, or the celebration of individuals who have served the church well and are now ending their time in it, we need to celebrate evidences of God's grace.

After all, there can be no order in community life unless we know where all good things come from. If you've reached a mile-marker, it's not because of your goodness, your faithfulness, or your consistency. If it had not been for the goodness of God that brought you through, you wouldn't be what you are. "Every good and every perfect gift is from above, coming down from the Father of lights" (James 1:17). We have to learn how to celebrate him with a thankful spirit.

The text does not tell us how long after the completion of the wall the dedication took place. We can assume it was very soon. Nehemiah did not separate the secular (wall building) from the sacred (worship); it was all part of the community's dedication of themselves to God. It was natural and appropriate to call a special worship service at the completion of the wall-building project that God had guided and protected.

Jerusalem is beginning to become the city of God again—not just in the geography, but in the people. They are the city on a hill—

a radiant community and nation, displaying the glory of Yahweh to all the nations.

Maybe that call to represent God is one reason why this celebration is so big. The people of God get the singers together from all the villages (Nehemiah **12:27-29**). Everyone's there. There are cymbals, harps, and lyres—they're going to make as much noise as they can.

When everyone's assembled, Nehemiah sends up two huge choirs onto the wall—one to the south and one to the north (**v 31, 38**). The leaders and the people are likewise split in two, one half on each side of the city. They're all standing on this wall, which they have repaired with their own hands.

The whole city is surrounded with singing. **Verse 43** sums up the feeling as the grand processions come to their fulfilment: joy. The word is used five times in one verse. They "rejoiced, for God had made them rejoice with great joy; the women and children also rejoiced. And the joy of Jerusalem was heard far away."

Restoration and reconciliation between God and his people should always be celebrated. When a sinner comes to God, there is feasting in heaven. Let's feast on earth too—and make sure that our joy in what the Lord has done can be heard even by those who are far away.

Questions for reflection

1. Think about your roles in work and family life. What would it look like for spiritual things to be at the heart of these structures? What steps can you take to make that happen?

2. Do you tend to separate the secular from the sacred in your life? How can you dedicate all of your life to God?

3. How good are you at celebrating what the Lord has done?

10. FAITH WITHOUT COMPROMISE

No matter how much a leader completes and accomplishes, managing difficult people is tough. The ending to the book of Nehemiah is filled with that reality.

In **12:44 – 13:3** we find out two more things that happened on the day when the wall was dedicated. First of all, worship made the people willing to serve (**12:44-47**). "On that day"—on the very same day that the choirs sang in Jerusalem—"men were appointed over the storerooms, the contributions, the firstfruits, and the tithes, to gather into them the portions required by the Law for the priests and for the Levites according to the fields of the towns, for Judah rejoiced over the priests and the Levites who ministered" (**v 44**).

The worship motivates the people. They rejoice in the priests and the Levites, who are leading the worship, and so they make plans for how they will make sure those men are paid to keep doing what they are doing. They have already promised to give tithes and contributions back in 10:32-39, but now they are appointing people to organize it all. They are figuring out how to actually plug in the order that God has commanded and get it to work.

By speaking of "the days of David and Asaph" (**12:46**), this passage harks back to 1 Chronicles 23 – 26. Here, as **David** grew old and planned to transition the kingdom to the rule of his son Solomon, he made sure that the order of the priesthood was in place for continued commitment to the Lord—commitment that would last throughout his son's reign and hopefully among later generations. An entire four chapters of 1 Chronicles are devoted to how David set up the organization of the various temple officials—in comparison with one chapter (1 Chronicles 27) where he organizes military matters. David was extravagant in his commitment to excellence in the corporate worship of God. From singers to gatekeepers to temple servants, these lists display David's concern that worship take place as it was supposed to.

Both in David's time and in Nehemiah's, there was meticulous order put into worship. Everything was thought through and accounted for—every ritual, every role. Reading this passage makes me pray that in today's church we won't be haphazard in our **liturgy** and corporate worship. Care for God's glory should mean that excellence in execution matters to us.

Yet ultimately, we should see this passage as having application well beyond our worship gatherings and music. It sheds light on how we function as a church in general. God's role for Israel was for them to be a whole kingdom of priests: a light to the nations, drawing them back to Yahweh (Exodus 19:6). That's our task too (Revelation 5:9-10). The meticulousness we see for the setting up of the priesthood can therefore apply to everything we do for the Lord. We should be drawing people to God not only through our church services and events but also through our everyday words and actions. That means we need to be meticulous in all those things.

We need to be active players, not benchwarmers, in God's church.

The willingness of the people to serve and to give is also a challenge for us today. Everyone is actively involved in some way. Likewise, we need to make sure we are not benchwarmers in God's church but active players in the team.

Sadly, though, many of us are on the team, but don't contribute anything. Maybe you're sick or you need some time out. Maybe you do need to take a rest and pull back from some things. But that doesn't mean not serving or contributing at all. There's no season of your life when you can't contribute in some way. We all need to prayerfully consider what we can give and how we can serve.

Next, the people read from the Scriptures again, just like they did in Nehemiah 8, and they're rocked by what the Lord has said: Ammonites and Moabites are not allowed to be part of the assembly of God (**13:1-3**).

These two peoples had a long history of opposing God's people. These verses refer to the time when the Moabites sought to utilize a man name Balaam against Israel (Numbers 22 – 24). They wanted him to curse God's people. Balaam went to the Moabite king, but he could not curse Israel. "Must I not take care to speak what the LORD puts in my mouth?" he explained (Numbers 23:12). This attempt to curse the Israelites—and other decisions like it—had a long-lasting influence on the Ammonites and Moabites. As a people, they remained fundamentally opposed to God. This is why they are not allowed in the assembly of God's people.

This removal of foreigners should not be viewed as racial exclusivism. As always, foreigners could become part of Israel by conversion (Ezra 6:21; Ruth 1:16–17). God is always most concerned about spiritual influence. He wanted his people to have families and a legacy that passed on kingdom commitment and ethics.

Tobiah in the Temple

But before all of this happened, we are told, something else took place—something that threatened the stability of the temple and the people's worship.

At some point, a priest named Eliashib had been appointed to govern the chambers of the temple. This Eliashib should not be identified with the high priest of the same name who served during Nehemiah's first tenure as governor of Judah. That Eliashib, in Nehemiah 3:1 and 20, is described as "the high priest"—but a high priest would not have been in charge of the storerooms. So this cannot be the same man (see Mervin Breneman, *Ezra, Nehemiah, Esther*, p 269).

Remember the contributions that were promised at the end of Nehemiah 10 and began to be made in **12:44**? All that was stored in a chamber in the temple. This was a small warehouse where they stored all of the ministry resources for the Levites and the leaders, so that they had what they needed to do what God had called them to do. And Eliashib was in charge of this chamber.

But Nehemiah went away, and as soon as he did, Eliashib went in there, took all of the resources out, and then gave the chamber to Tobiah as an apartment inside the temple of God.

Why does this matter? First of all, Tobiah was an Ammonite (2:10). Note the connection with the previous verses (**13:1-3**)! He was not even supposed to be in the temple at all. Second, we know that he was a nonbeliever. He did not like the people of God.

In 2:10 Tobiah sought his personal welfare, not that of the people of God. In 2:19 and 4:3, he challenged the value of God's work in Jerusalem. In 4:7 he was angry because the development of Jerusalem was destroying his influence. In 6:1-2 he made plans to destroy Nehemiah. In 6:3-4 he resented Nehemiah for not acknowledging his and Sanballat's self-perceived importance. He also tried to persuade Nehemiah to abandon the work of God to tend to his personal selfish desires. In 6:5-7, Tobiah tried to undermine Nehemiah's leadership and the credibility of the work of God by attempting to build a false case against his motives. He then used Shemaiah's false theology to try to get at Nehemiah and give him a bad name (6:12-13).

This was the man who was now set up with his own apartment in the temple! Tobiah was a key person in the opposition to Nehemiah's reforms—and Eliashib had now given him a foothold right in the center of the Jewish community.

That's not the only problem. This apartment was inside the temple—which was supposed to be the place where the presence of God was. Of course, God dwells in heaven. There is nothing made with human hands that can hold him. But in Old Testament times he gave an expression of his presence on earth. The temple represented the fact that God was with his people. "I will make my dwelling among you," he said (Leviticus 26:11). The temple was where God lived! But they had put Tobiah in there. They had taken the dwelling of God and turned it into a dwelling of divisiveness.

It's not surprising. Whenever God sets stuff in order among the people of God, the enemy will try to disrupt and come against it. The enemy always wants to reverse God's order, to manipulate it, and to control it.

If I am spending too much time on something that is not what God wants me to spend time on, I have got a Tobiah in my life. Tobiah is a leech. When a Tobiah is in your life, you're always trying to make him feel comfortable. "What do you need, Tobiah? Do you need some food, something to drink, Tobiah? What do you want me to do, Tobiah?" He will have us serving him instead of God.

Reading about Tobiah should prompt us to ask ourselves: what things in my life are out of order? Maybe it's relationships with friends. Maybe it's family relationships. Maybe your finances or your spiritual life are out of order. The enemy tries to disrupt our lives so that God won't get the glory that he's supposed to get. We must challenge the enemy and get things back under God's divine order. We must throw Tobiah out.

Holy Indignant

This disaster with Tobiah happened because Nehemiah was away (**13:6**). In Nehemiah 2, Artaxerxes gave his support and resources to Nehemiah so that the people could rebuild the walls. But Nehemiah had to promise to return (2:6). He had to go back and fulfill that requirement by staying with the king for a while.

But now Nehemiah returned to Jerusalem, and he was distressed (**13:8**). For all Nehemiah's efforts in regard to maintaining ceremonial and religious purity, those whom he'd left behind in leadership had let things slide to a serious degree. The high priest must have known about the matter with Tobiah and even permitted it. Eliashib had been given a job—to be in charge of the storerooms of the temple—but he had shown a serious lack of responsibility, which allowed Tobiah to gain more and more influence in the community.

In leadership there is delegation, and in delegation there must be trust. If a leader gives people influence and they use it to strengthen God's enemies, this can destroy everything that the leader is trying to build. Satan will use people to destroy the mission and work of God.

That means that every now and then we need to get "holy indignant." When we see a gap between where God wants things and where things are, it is not a time to be polite! When Jesus went into the court of the temple and saw that it had been turned into a marketplace, he didn't say, *Oh, well, please listen to me...* He got angry. He started turning tables over (Mark 11:15).

There are things in our lives that we need to turn over, too. I'm not just talking about removing bad influences in the church. Yes, we should remove from positions of authority those who do not display the kind of godliness the New Testament demands. But the relevance here is wider than that. I'm talking about anything at all that leads us away from God. There are things in our lives we shouldn't be nice about. If there's something disrupting God's order, we need to throw it out. Just like Nehemiah did, literally: "I was very angry, and I threw all the household furniture of Tobiah out of the chamber" (Nehemiah **13:8**).

We must remove anything that has disrupted God's divine order. Remove it today. There's no mission of God that can go forward until that happens.

I've learned this in my life personally. There have been some things and people and places that I wanted more than God wanted. If I don't remove those things, God will do it—and it's always rougher when God removes them. He wants us to be like Jesus. Romans 8:29 tells us we were made for this purpose. At the end of the day, it's about the image of Christ. And that's going to hurt sometimes.

But it's not just about removing sin and disruption. We need to understand and re-establish God's original order. In Mark 11:17, Jesus said that his Father's house should be a house of prayer. He understood God's original purpose. Likewise, Nehemiah knows what God's order looks like, and he reestablishes it. He tells us in Nehemiah **13:9**, "I gave orders, and they cleansed the chambers, and I brought back there the vessels of the house of God, with the grain offering and the frankincense."

Through the blood of Christ, we can cleanse the chamber of our souls. And then we can say, "God helped me to put this back in place." This is what it means to "work out your own salvation"—not for it (Philippians 2:12). It's not a moralistic effort. It's the strength we gain through the power of the gospel. We are living out the righteousness that Christ already bought on the cross for us. We can look to him to see what that righteousness involves, and then we can ask for his help in putting our souls in order.

Questions for reflection

1. Do you contribute at church? If not, is there something small you could start doing to serve others?

2. Is there anything in your life that is out of order? What needs to change? Who could you ask to help you?

3. What kinds of things do you think God wants us to be "holy indignant" about? Can you back up your answer with a Bible reference?

PART TWO

Broken Promises

Tobiah's apartment in the temple is not the only problem Nehemiah encounters when he gets back to Jerusalem. In fact, the people have compromised on all the commitments that that they made in chapter 10.

First comes the promise of tithes to support the work in the temple. Nehemiah reports, "I also found out that the portions of the Levites had not been given to them, so that the Levites and the singers, who did the work, had fled each to his field" (**13:10**).

So he sorts it out. "I gathered them together and set them in their stations. Then all Judah brought the tithe of the grain, wine, and oil into the storehouses" (**v 11-12**). He also appoints treasurers—people who looked after the money: "Shelemiah the priest, Zadok the scribe, and Pedaiah of the Levites, and as their assistant Hanan the son of Zaccar, son of Mattaniah" (**v 13**). He chooses them because "they were considered reliable."

Nehemiah has been stung by his experience with Eliashib. He needs people who have a track record of reliability, who can set a standard for what it means to be faithful to the living God. He starts with the treasurers because money is usually where a lack of reliability starts.

Reliability means to prove firm, to be faithful and loyal. It has the idea of certainty; you're not fickle and all over the place. You're sure about what you're doing, and you'll endure when the going gets tough.

Reliability is a weighty biblical requirement. If a person is committed to the local church, that is weighty. If a person is committed to a spouse, that is weighty. If we raise our children in the fear and admonition of the Lord, it is weighty. If we go to work on time, if we pay our bills on time, it is weighty. It is significant. It is living the way God wants us to live. It is being like God, who is always faithful.

The paying of tithes isn't the only promise God's people have broken. Secondly, they have stopped keeping the Sabbath.

"In those days I saw in Judah people treading the winepresses
on the Sabbath, and bringing in heaps of grain and loading
them on donkeys, and also wine, grapes, figs, and all kinds of
loads, which they brought into Jerusalem on the Sabbath day.
And I warned them on the day when they sold food. Tyrians
also, who lived in the city, brought in fish and all kinds of goods
and sold them on the Sabbath to the people of Judah, in Jerusalem itself!" (**v 15-16**)

You can see Nehemiah's indignation at once. He is outraged by their
brazen flouting of God's laws.

The people who were buying and selling food would probably say,
*We're not working. We're letting people that are not of God work for
us.* In other words, they have lost the spirit of the Sabbath. The Sabbath is about rest; but central to the idea of rest is trusting in God. The
people have stopped believing that God will provide.

But Nehemiah is in no doubt as to the sin of what they're doing. He
confronts them (**v 17-18**), reminding them of the sins of their fathers,
which we saw them confess in chapter 9. Now they're doing the same
thing, he tells them—and they're bound to bring more wrath on Israel.

With that in mind, Nehemiah puts in place a hard and drastic stop
(**13:19-22**). Some changes you can't afford to wait on; you have to
implement them as soon as possible. Nehemiah issues an order that
the gates of the city are to be closed from late afternoon just before
the Sabbath until after the holy day is over—so, probably from about
5pm on Friday to about 11am on Sunday morning (compare 7:3).
He then posts some of his servants, probably men from his personal
military entourage, at the gates to ensure that no load can be brought
in on the Sabbath.

Evidently believing that the situation is temporary, the traders and
merchants spend the night outside Jerusalem a few times. Nehemiah
then threatens them with physical force, warning the traders and merchants to stay away from the city during the Sabbath. The warning
works. From that time forward, the traders and merchants do not

come to Jerusalem during the holy day. This means that there can be a sense of rest without the pressure or temptation of finances leading anyone to justify breaking the Sabbath.

All of us need unpressured rest. When I go on **sabbatical**, it takes two weeks to shut off. I unplug from all work-related items in order to be comprehensively replenished. This is why Jesus said that the Sabbath is for man. Rest is not just a meaningless command—it is for our good. It is a vital discipline that keeps us centered on God in all of life. It is serious that the people have broken this promise, and that's why Nehemiah acts so decisively.

Thirdly, the people have reneged on their promise not to allow their sons or daughters to marry unbelievers. "Also I saw the Jews who had married women of Ashdod, Ammon, and Moab. And half of their children spoke the language of Ashdod, and they could not speak the language of Judah, but only the language of each people" (**13:23-24**). That's a big deal because these children can't understand the Scriptures. They speak the language of the peoples around them instead of the language of God's people. They have a deeper connection to the people of **pagan** cultures than to the people of God.

This gets Nehemiah even more angry than he has been already—not with the children or the foreign wives but with the Jewish men who have broken their oath. "I confronted them and cursed them and beat some of them and pulled out their hair."

Can you imagine this happening today? Can you imagine somebody getting beaten up because they're not following the Lord? Their beards pulled out? We shouldn't do that, but we should have the passion that Nehemiah has for his people. He is not getting angry for his own sake. He is getting angry for their sake.

The Bible doesn't seem to judge the response of Nehemiah as good or bad—though this isn't exactly an encouragement to marry outside the faith today. The focus here is more on Israel and the importance of turning back to covenantal faithfulness. We do need to disciple people well not to compromise God's word for the sake of their personal preferences.

Nehemiah's Greatest Fear

In **verse 26**, Nehemiah explains himself: "Did not Solomon king of Israel sin on account of such women?"

Solomon was the greatest king of his generation, the wisest man who had ever lived (1 Kings 3:12), beloved by his God. Yet even he fell into sin when his foreign wives led him astray. To me, one of the most haunting verses in the Bible is 1 Kings 11:4. "When Solomon was old his wives turned away his heart after other gods, and his heart was not wholly true to the LORD his God, as was the heart of David his father." This is my greatest fear, and it's Nehemiah's too.

The fact is that our hearts can get compromised. Good organization and structure are all great. Being exposed to great information is amazing. But you can have those things and still not have a heart that is shaped by God. And that can have catastrophic consequences. Solomon is a picture of what it looks like to serve God with only half a heart. He had a Tobiah in the temple: a harem of foreign women who led him astray. He thought it would be fine to marry women who worshiped other gods, as long as he himself remained faithful. But he couldn't remain faithful with those women in his life. He loved them, and he started to love their gods, too. When he married them, he was allowing his devotion to God to be compromised.

Nehemiah doesn't want that to happen to him or his people. He recognizes these marriages for what they are: treachery against God (Nehemiah **13:27**). This is why he has acted with such anger against these men.

God is the only one Nehemiah wants to please. Look at **verses 14, 22, 29**, and **31**. "Remember me, O my God … Remember this also in my favor, O my God … Remember me, O my God, for good." Nehemiah seems to have something that many others lack: intimacy with God and commitment to his will. When he is around to manage people, they are fine, but when he isn't, they fall into error. He doesn't want to fall into error himself, so he prays these brief staccato prayers out of a disposition of trust in the Lord and as a plea for his continued favor.

Nehemiah has thrown out Tobiah, appointed reliable people, re-established the Sabbath, and railed against those who have disobeyed God. In the final verses of Nehemiah 13 he chases away one last enemy (**v 28**) and acts again to cleanse the people of God and to establish the work of the temple (**v 30-31**). He is uncompromising in his determination to lead his people to walk in God's ways.

The Return of the King

Nehemiah 13 provides an interesting connection with Jesus. Just as Nehemiah went back to his king to stay with him for a while, and then returned to check on the state of his people, so Jesus Christ left earth after he was raised from the grave and went up to the right hand of his King. He's sitting interceding for us, pushing for us, looking out for us. But he's going to return once again. What will he find?

We should all be asking ourselves that question. Will we be like the ten virgins who were ready with their lamps, or the ones who had given up and got bored (Matthew 25:1-13)? Will we be like the servant who invested his master's money well, or will we be like the one who hid it in the ground and pretended it didn't exist (Matthew 25:14-30)? Are we serving and representing Jesus with the best of our ability?

Today's Mission

As I think about all that is going on in my society, I believe the themes and theology of Nehemiah can be an amazing help. Nehemiah is a case study about the people of God getting themselves ready by the grace and power of God to be a light again. The light had been lost but was now being restored. We, too, as the church in the world, need to ensure we are a light.

Nehemiah helps us with having vision. He shows us how to see God's work of redemption on every level—in society and in the practicalities of people's lives, as well as in their souls. That helps us to develop an awareness of the deep work of God, even as we get on the ground and focus on the details of real-life situations.

Nehemiah shows us that we can resist the enemy and be productive even when he is attempting to short-circuit God's kingdom plans. This book inspires us to see opportunities to rebuild broken communities—putting God's word at the center of community life in and through the church.

As the church, we must see our work as discipling the whole person. The gospel doesn't single out just spiritual or just physical needs and speak to those. Christian community development begins with people transformed by the love of God, who then respond to God's call to share the gospel with others through evangelism, social action, economic development, and justice. These groups of Christians start churches and community-development corporations, evangelism outreaches and tutoring programs, discipleship groups and housing programs, prayer groups and businesses.

We need to know how to defend our faith to others verbally. But to see transformation in our cities, in our culture, and in our time, we also need the power-packed, missional tool of a godly lifestyle.

> Building under God isn't easy. But it is worth it.

In other words, we need to be a people of uncompromised faith. We need to live a life that's uncompromised and committed wholeheartedly to the Lord Jesus Christ.

Building under God isn't an easy task. It involves praying for God's hand to work, having clear vision, resisting opposition and distractions, putting honorable order in place, and correcting those who constantly compromise the greater mission. But it is worth it.

Jesus is building a new Jerusalem, where one day both Jews and Gentiles will be present as equals. God will make his tabernacle among us, and we will reign with him forever. All will be in order: the new Jerusalem will be the headquarters of the eternal kingdom of God forever and ever.

Ultimately it's not our own projects here on earth that we're building toward. It's God's eternal project, God's eternal city. That's our sure and certain future. That's what we are representing to the world around us today—like a city on a hill, which cannot be hidden (Matthew 5:14).

Questions for reflection

1. Are you reliable? How could you grow in this trait?

2. What does it look like to be uncompromising in our passion for the Lord? What are some good ways of expressing this?

3. How has Nehemiah refreshed your vision for the church? What practical things will you go away and do as a result of reading this book?

GLOSSARY

Abram: another name for **Abraham** (see below, and Genesis 17:5).

Abraham: the ancestor of the nation of Israel, and the man God made a covenant (a binding agreement) with. God promised to make his family into a great nation, give them a land, and bring blessing to all nations through one of his descendants (see Genesis 12:1-3).

Anoint: to specifically choose or send. In Old Testament times, kings were anointed instead of crowned. Their foreheads were smeared with oil, which is the literal meaning of the word "anoint."

Apostles: the men who were appointed directly by the risen Christ to teach about him with authority.

Attribute: a characteristic or trait. God's attributes include being all-powerful, all-knowing, and perfectly good.

Blasphemy: when God is disrespected or mocked.

Cast lots: make a decision based on a seemingly random outcome, like the toss of a coin. (However, in the Old Testament, casting lots with the Urim and Thummim was a God-given way of receiving his guidance.)

Chattel slavery: when people are owned as property.

Circumcised: a man or boy whose foreskin has been cut off. God told the men among his people in the Old Testament to be circumcised as a way to show physically that they knew and trusted him and belonged to the people of God (see Genesis 17).

Commentator: the author of a commentary, a book that explains parts of the Bible verse by verse.

Convicted: convinced. Being convicted of sin means being brought to a fresh awareness of one's own sin. This should lead to repentance.

Cornerstone: the most important stone in a building.

Covenant: a binding agreement or promise. In the Bible, the old covenant set out how believers in the Old Testament related to God;

Jesus established the new covenant, so believers now relate to God through his saving death and resurrection.

David: the second king of Israel, and the most important king in Old Testament history. He also wrote many of the psalms.

Day of Atonement: the one day in the year when a priest could enter the Most Holy Place in the temple to make a sacrifice on behalf of the people, as a sign that they were being cleansed of their sins (Leviticus 16).

Deity: being God.

Edify: build someone up by teaching or encouraging them.

Eschatological: relating to death, judgment and eternity.

Ethical: to do with how you should behave.

Evangelicals: Christians who, broadly speaking, emphasize the importance of personal conversion through faith and recognize the authority of the Bible.

Exodus: the historical period when the people of Israel left slavery in Egypt and began to travel toward the **promised land**. It literally means "way out" or "departure."

Fall: the moment when Eve and Adam disobeyed God and ate from the tree of the knowledge of good and evil (see Genesis 3).

Fasting: not eating for a set period. This can help fuel prayer.

Feast of Booths: a Jewish festival in which people build and live in temporary shelters (or booths), to remember the **exodus**. This is known in modern times as Sukkot. See pages 115-117.

Gentiles: non-Jews.

Gospel: the proclamation that Jesus was God himself; that he died for sins; that he rose to rule and give new life; that he is reigning in heaven and will return to restore the world. Gospel mission is anything that promotes this message.

Grace: undeserved favor. In the Bible, "grace" is usually used to describe how God treats his people. Because God is full of grace, he gives believers eternal life (Ephesians 2:4-8); he also gives them gifts to use to serve his people (Ephesians 4:7, 11-13).

Heathen: here meaning non-Jewish.

Incarnation: the coming of the divine Son of God as a human, in the person of Jesus Christ.

Intercession: speaking on someone else's behalf (especially in prayer).

Jeshua: another spelling of Joshua, the man who led God's people into the **promised land**.

Jonah: a man sent by God to the city of Nineveh, bringing a message from God telling the people there to repent.

Jubilee law: a set of rules which involved restoring property to its original owners and allowing the land to rest. See Leviticus 25.

Judah: the southern part of the **promised land**. After the rule of **Solomon**, God's people split into two nations: Israel and Judah. Judah tended to have leaders who were more obedient to God. The capital of Judah was Jerusalem.

Judges: leaders of God's people in the period after they settled in the **promised land** but before they had kings.

Levites: members of the tribe of Levi, one of the twelve tribes of Israel. Levites served as priests and temple servants.

Liturgy: the order and language of a church service.

Ministry: the work of someone who cares for others. It includes preaching and teaching about Jesus as well as caring for physical needs.

Missiologist: someone who studies the strategies and history of Christian mission (the work of spreading the word about Jesus).

Pagan: here meaning non-Jewish.

Parable: a memorable story that illustrates a truth about Jesus or his kingdom.

Pentecost: originally a Jewish feast celebrating God giving his people his law on Mount Sinai (Exodus 19 – 31). On the day of this feast, fifty days after Jesus' resurrection, the Holy Spirit came to the first Christians (Acts 2), so "Pentecost" is how Christians tend to refer to this event.

Priest: someone who represents people to God.

Promised land: the land on the eastern coast of the Mediterranean Sea which God promised to give to **Abraham**'s descendants (Genesis 12:6-8; 13:14-18), and which the Israelites eventually took possession of under the leadership of Joshua.

Propitiation: appeasing someone's anger at wrongdoing.

Providence: the all-powerful care of God, who oversees everything that happens and directs events for the good of his people.

Redemption: freeing or releasing someone from slavery by buying them for a price. The word is used in the Bible to show how, by dying on the cross, Christ released us from slavery to sin and death.

Redlining: denying certain services (especially financial services) to those who live in particular areas, based on their race or ethnicity.

Revelation: when God reveals himself or a truth about himself.

Sabbatical: a period of paid leave from work, often used for study or travel.

Saints: a biblical term for all Christians.

Sanctify: to make holy or make more like Christ, by the work of the Holy Spirit.

Satisfaction: paying a debt in full or completely fulfilling an obligation.

Scribe: in Bible times, a scholar and expert in God's word.

Solomon: the king who succeeded **David**. He built the temple in Jerusalem and was renowned for his wisdom.

Son of Man: a title Jesus used for himself, drawn from Daniel 7:13.

Sovereignty: supreme authority and total control.

Steward: someone who looks after something on behalf of someone else.

Synagogue: a local place of worship, prayer and teaching for Jewish people.

Temple: the center of life and worship for God's people in the Old Testament. Located in Jerusalem.

The lost: a term for non-Christians, drawn from Luke 19:10.

Theology: the study of what is true about God, or a particular understanding or interpretation of what is true about God.

Torah: the five books of Moses in the Jewish Scriptures (Genesis, Exodus, Leviticus, Numbers and Deuteronomy).

Transcendent: far above what is humanly possible.

Trial: a difficult or testing period of life.

Vocational ministry: full-time Christian work.

Wilderness: the wild or desert region which God's people wandered in after leaving slavery in Egypt and before reaching the **promised land**.

Wrath: God's settled, deserved hatred of and anger at sin.

Yahweh: the name by which God revealed himself to Moses (Exodus 3:13-14). Literally, it means "I am who I am" or "I will be who I will be." Most English-language Bibles translate it as "LORD", using small capital letters.

BIBLIOGRAPHY

■ Clinton E. Arnold, *Three Crucial Questions about Spiritual Warfare* (Baker, 1997).

■ Vince Bantu, *A Multitude of All Peoples: Engaging Ancient Christianity's Global Identity* (IVP, 2020).

■ Lois Barrett / Darrell L. Guder et al., *Missional Church: A Vision for the Sending of the Church in North America* (Eerdmans, 1998).

■ Mervin Breneman, *Ezra, Nehemiah, Esther* (Broadman & Holman, 1993).

■ F. Charles Fensham, *The Books of Ezra and Nehemiah* (Eerdmans, 1982).

■ Gillis Gerleman, *Esther* (Neukirchen-Vluyn, 1973).

■ Gregory Goswell, "Ezra–Nehemiah," in *The Baker Illustrated Bible Background Commentary,* ed. J. Scott Duvall and J. Daniel Hays (Baker Books, 2020).

■ J. Daniel Hays, *From Every People and Nation: A Biblical Theology of Race* (IVP, 2003).

■ Anthony A. Hoekema, *Saved by Grace* (Eerdmans, 1994).

■ F. C. Holmgren, *Ezra and Nehemiah: Israel Alive Again* (Eerdmans, 1996).

■ Kathleen Kenyon, *Digging up Jerusalem* (Praeger, 1974).

■ Martin Luther King, *Letter from a Birmingham Jail* (1963).

■ Doug Logan, *On the Block: Developing a Biblical Picture for Missional Engagement* (Moody, 2016).

■ Israel Loken, *Ezra & Nehemiah* (Lexham Press, 2011).

▪ Victor Harold Matthews, Mark W. Chavalas, and John H. Walton, *The IVP Bible Background Commentary: Old Testament* (IVP, 2000).

▪ Manuel Ortiz and Harvie M. Conn, *Urban Ministry: The Kingdom, the City and the People of God* (IVP, 2010).

▪ John M. Perkins, *Restoring At-Risk Communities: Doing It Together and Doing It Right* (Baker, 1996).

▪ Alexander Strauch, *Biblical Eldership: An Urgent Call to Restore Biblical Church Leadership* (Lewis & Roth, 1995)

▪ John H. Walton, *1 & 2 Kings, 1 & 2 Chronicles, Ezra, Nehemiah, Esther* (Zondervan, 2009).

▪ John H. Walton, *Zondervan Illustrated Bible Backgrounds Commentary: Old Testament,* volume 3 (Zondervan, 2009).

▪ Thomas B. White, *The Believer's Guide to Spiritual Warfare* (Chosen Books, 2011).

▪ H.G.M. Williamson, *Ezra, Nehemiah* (Thomas Nelson, 1985).

Nehemiah for...

Bible-study Groups

Eric Mason's *Good Book Guide* to Nehemiah is the companion to this resource, helping groups of Christians to explore, discuss, and apply the messages of this book together. Eight studies, each including investigation, application, getting personal, prayer and explore more sections, take you through the book of Nehemiah. Includes a concise Leader's Guide at the back.

Nehemiah
God's building project

8 studies   by Eric Mason

Find out more at:
www.thegoodbook.com/goodbookguides
www.thegoodbook.co.uk/goodbookguides

Daily Devotionals

Explore daily devotional helps you open up the Scriptures and will encourage and equip you in your walk with God. Available as a quarterly booklet, *Explore* is also available as an app, where you can download Eric's notes on Nehemiah, alongside contributions from trusted Bible teachers including Tim Keller, Sam Allberry, Albert Mohler, and David Helm.

Find out more at:
www.thegoodbook.com/explore
www.thegoodbook.co.uk/explore

The Whole Series

- **Exodus For You** *Tim Chester*

- **Judges For You** *Timothy Keller*

- **Ruth For You** *Tony Merida*

- **1 Samuel For You** *Tim Chester*

- **2 Samuel For You** *Tim Chester*

- **Psalms For You** *Christopher Ash*

- **Proverbs For You** *Kathleen Nielson*

- **Isaiah For You** *Tim Chester*

- **Daniel For You** *David Helm*

- **Micah For You** *Stephen Um*

- **Luke 1-12 For You** *Mike McKinley*

- **Luke 12-24 For You** *Mike McKinley*

- **John 1-12 For You** *Josh Moody*

- **John 13-21 For You** *Josh Moody*

- **Acts 1-12 For You** *Albert Mohler*

- **Acts 13-28 For You** *Albert Mohler*

- **Romans 1-7 For You** *Timothy Keller*

- **Romans 8-16 For You** *Timothy Keller*

- **1 Corinthians For You** *Andrew Wilson*

- **2 Corinthians For You** *Gary Millar*

- **Galatians For You** *Timothy Keller*

- **Ephesians For You** *Richard Coekin*

- **Philippians For You** *Steven Lawson*

- **Colossians & Philemon For You**
  Mark Meynell

- **1 & 2 Timothy For You** *Phillip Jensen*

- **Titus For You** *Tim Chester*

- **Hebrews For You** *Michael Kruger*

- **James For You** *Sam Allberry*

- **1 Peter For You** *Juan Sanchez*

- **2 Peter & Jude For You** *Miguel Núñez*

- **Revelation For You** *Tim Chester*

Find out more about these resources at:
www.thegoodbook.com/for-you
www.thegoodbook.co.uk/for-you

BIBLICAL | RELEVANT | ACCESSIBLE

At The Good Book Company, we are dedicated to helping Christians and local churches grow. We believe that God's growth process always starts with hearing clearly what he has said to us through his timeless word—the Bible.

Ever since we opened our doors in 1991, we have been striving to produce Bible-based resources that bring glory to God. We have grown to become an international provider of user-friendly resources to the Christian community, with believers of all backgrounds and denominations using our books, Bible studies, devotionals, evangelistic resources, and DVD-based courses.

We want to equip ordinary Christians to live for Christ day by day, and churches to grow in their knowledge of God, their love for one another, and the effectiveness of their outreach.

Call us for a discussion of your needs or visit one of our local websites for more information on the resources and services we provide.

Your friends at The Good Book Company

thegoodbook.com | thegoodbook.co.uk
thegoodbook.com.au | thegoodbook.co.nz
thegoodbook.co.in